Renovating Your Writing

SHAPING IDEAS INTO CLEAR, CONCISE, AND COMPELLING MESSAGES

Renovating Your Writing

SHAPING IDEAS INTO CLEAR, CONCISE, AND COMPELLING MESSAGES

Richard Kallan
California State Polytechnic University, Pomona

Boston   Columbus   Indianapolis   New York   San Francisco   Upper Saddle River   Amsterdam
Cape Town   Dubai   London   Madrid   Milan   Munich   Paris   Montreal   Toronto   Delhi
Mexico City   Sao Paulo   Sydney   Hong Kong   Seoul   Singapore   Taipei   Tokyo

Editor-in-Chief, Communication: Karon Bowers
Assistant Editor: Stephanie Chaisson
Editorial Assistant: Megan Sweeney
Production Project Manager: Elizabeth Gale Napolitano
Marketing Manager: Blair Zoe Tuckman
Project Coordination and Text Design: Niraj Bhatt/Aptara®, Inc.
Manager, Central Design: Jayne Conte
Cover Designer: Axell Design
Cover Image: Andres Rodrigez/Alamy

Credits and acknowledgments borrowed from other sources and reproduced, with permission, in this textbook appear on appropriate page.

Many of the designations by manufacturers and sellers to distinguish their products are claimed as trademarks. Where those designations appear in this book, and the publisher was aware of a trademark claim, the designations have been printed in initial caps or all caps.

Library of Congress Cataloging-in-Publication Data

Kallan, Richard A.
    Renovating your writing : shaping ideas into clear, concise, and compelling messages / Richard Kallan.
        p. cm.
    Includes index.
    ISBN-13: 978-0-205-25439-2
    ISBN-10: 0-205-25439-X
    1. English language—Rhetoric.   2. Composition (Language arts)   I. Title.
    PE1408 .K257
    808' .042—dc23   2011049182

ISBN-13: 978-0-205-25439-2
ISBN-10:   0-205-25439-X

For Daniel Kallan, my father, and Jerry Novotny, my high school newspaper advisor, who took turns teaching me how to write a *sentence;* and Robert D. Brooks, director of my master's thesis, who showed me how to craft a *paragraph.* Guided by the lessons of these mentors, I am still working on the *page.*

CONTENTS

NOTE

Some portions of this book originally appeared in Robert Gunning and Richard Kallan, *How to Take the Fog Out of Business Writing* (Chicago: Dartnell, 1994); Richard Kallan, "Teaching Journalistic Cogency with 55-Word Short Stories," *Journalism & Mass Communication Educator* 55.3 (2000), adapted with permission; and Richard Kallan, "Thoughts on Right Way to Write" and "Weigh Letter of Application Carefully," guest columns, published concurrently in *Pasadena Star-News, San Gabriel Valley Tribune,* and *Whittier Daily News* May 12, 2008 and May 19, 2008.

ACKNOWLEDGMENTS

From first draft to final manuscript, *Renovating Your Writing* benefited keenly from the advice of Karon Bowers, the close reading of Darla Anderson, and the comments and suggestions of the following reviewers:

Jeffrey Brand, *Millikin University*

Daniel R. Fredrick, *American University of Sharjah*

Patricia S. Hill, *The University of Akron*

Lawrence A. Hosman, *University of Southern Mississippi*

John Levine, *UC Berkeley*

Daryle Nagano, *El Camino College*

Esther Rumsey, *Sul Ross State University*

PART I

Strategies, Tactics, and Tips

1 Rethinking Your Thoughts About Writing

Ill-conceived, badly executed writing appears everywhere. And it exacts a steep price. Consider these common scenarios:

- A ponderous report about how to improve campus parking is set aside because it is unreadable, resulting in vital information being ignored.
- An imprecise e-mail to a classmate working on a group project spurs the opposite action intended, wasting time and misdirecting the group's focus.
- An unclear letter to an employer is so confusing that it requires another letter to correct its mistakes, leading to more work and a potentially strained relationship.
- A poorly organized term paper casts the author as unknowledgeable, when quite the opposite is true.

Renovating Your Writing: Shaping Ideas into Clear, Concise, and Compelling Messages helps remedy these problems. The strategies, tactics, and tips presented serve as a blueprint for developing the skills needed to effectively self-revise your writing. These skills allow you to transform untamed thought into clear, concise, and compelling messages.

All too often, writing instruction fails to provide guidelines that are both practical *and* nuanced; absent are lessons that can be adapted to a host of different writing situations. In contrast, *Renovating Your Writing* offers a more layered approach to guide you. It is not a beginner's book about how to choose a topic, access databases and research tools, or evaluate information. Instead, it is aimed at writers experienced in expressing themselves who want to take their work to the next level.

All too often, writing instruction also fails to acknowledge, let alone discuss, the teaching and learning challenges that emanate from how you approach the writing process and how you perceive your own writing. Let's first look at the writing process.

THE WRITING PROCESS: SEPARATING FACT FROM FICTION

Most People Think They Should Like Writing

The notion that writing should be enjoyable began early in our schooling when well-meaning teachers sought to motivate us. Writing could be fun, they promised, once we knew enough to appreciate the art. Sadly, that is not the case. Worse, the fun standard trivializes the key requisite for good writing: hard work. Quality writing mandates time, energy, and a commitment to self-criticism and self-correction. For most writers, the payoff comes from achieving their purpose. The process can enlighten and gratify, but it is seldom a joy ride. To think otherwise is to approach writing unprepared for its demands.

Should you not find writing to be sheer ecstasy, do not despair; you are not alone. Personal journal writing can be enjoyable, but most other writing forms test our creative and organizational skills. Writing anything other than the simplest of messages can be taxing, frustrating, and stressful.

Moreover, it is okay not to like writing. Whether you do or don't does not matter any more than whether you like or dislike stopping at a red light. It is simply something you must learn—and learn well—to enhance your opportunities for professional success.

Most People Think They Can Improve Their Writing Skills by Simply Reading More and Writing More

After all, isn't that what every teacher has told us since day one? Under the right conditions, reading more and writing more can improve writing skills, but neither activity by itself will transform your writing.

First, it is what you read and *how* you read it that counts. Devouring fiction (novels, plays, poetry), whose purpose, structure, and style differ so markedly from nonfiction writing (memos, letters, reports, essays, term papers), may inspire creativity, but it will not teach you much about nonfiction writing. If it did, every voracious reader of such literature would be a great writer. All are not, and, in fact, most do not seem to write much better than their literature-averse counterparts. Nor will your writing improve by simply reading a lot of nonfiction—unless you choose quality nonfiction, and then, as you read, closely analyze the text and the choices the author makes. Obviously, this is seldom how anyone reads much of anything.

Second, you will not become a better writer just by writing more. One need only survey the millions of blogs faithfully produced everyday to realize that practice alone does not make perfect. The *informed* practice of rewriting, not the act of writing per se, improves writing skills. You must first know the principles of effective composition and then engage in constant revision and editing. In this way, writing is like any other accomplished skill: It is the product of knowledge, sustained practice, and ongoing evaluation and correction.

As you become a better writer, you may be surprised to learn that you are not also becoming a faster writer. Ironically, writing speed typically decreases with improved skills because the writer, better able to recognize and appreciate good writing, now has higher standards to meet. Additionally, the ease with which computers allow for rewriting slows the process because it is so tempting to keep revising and improving drafts.

Most People Think Their Writing Will Be Read by an Ideal Audience

Many of us assume that our messages will be read carefully by an *ideal* reader who eagerly awaits our every word. We create texts as if our audience were our adoring mom and dad, or perhaps our loving spouse or partner. We write for a perfectly attentive, perfectly perceptive, perfectly analytic audience—that rarely exists. More often, our readers are short on time and patience; overwhelmed with e-mails, proposals, and reports, many of which they would prefer not to read; and used to skipping and skimming nearly everything they read. They are not our mom and dad.

A better perspective, even when you know differently, is to assume that your reader is tired and cranky, bored by your subject, opposed to your position, and hostile toward you. When you write for this less-than-ideal reader, you are forced to focus on what is most important: getting the audience to read, understand, and accept your message. You lead with your best arguments, develop them more efficiently, and refrain from off-handed comments that usually are not all that clever or relevant. You stay more earnest, less apt to come across as cocky or boorish.

Realize that all writing is persuasive. Readers can never be taken for granted and must continually be courted. The writer first attempts to convince potential readers to read what is written. Aside from enticing titles and intriguing subject lines, documents that are visually inviting—easier and more interesting to read owing to their attractive layout and formatting—are more likely to beckon the audience's attention. Whether such messages continue to hold the audience's attention, and to what degree, is again a matter of readability—how clearly, concisely, and compellingly (well-organized and well-argued) the message comes across. Seen in this context, your writing proficiency functions foremost to secure and maintain your readers' attention.

When we say that all writing is persuasive, we also mean that all writing seeks to persuade its readers to believe and act upon what they read. Even the most descriptive of messages is persuasive in the sense that the writer tries to convince readers to accept the information as believable. The difference between asking your audience to vote for a specific candidate and describing the voting process is one of degree, not kind. In both cases, the writer's primary task is to present credible arguments or descriptions the reader can trust. In the former example, the call to action is explicit, while in the latter it is implicit insofar as beliefs lead to corollary behaviors. In other words, knowing about the voting process leads one to be more willing or less willing to vote. In both cases, however, your perceived trustworthiness, wrought by everything you do as a writer, is central to your persuasibility.

Finally, all writing functions persuasively and sometimes in unintended ways. Language evokes denotative and connotative meanings that lead readers to form beliefs and pursue actions, not all of which are designed by the writer. Even the simplest of descriptive ideas in the right context can cause unimagined effects. *I love starting my day with a huge steak-and-eggs breakfast* will be processed differently by a cardiac patient than by a college football player. Each will come away with an opposite view of the merits of your diet. Intent and function are not synonymous, which is why the road to Hell is paved with good intentions.

YOUR WRITING: SEPARATING FACT FROM FICTION

Most People Think They Write Better Than They Do

Academics, of course, lead the pack. Even when they pen something they admit is arduous to follow, it is never because of how it is written. Rather it is because the ideas expressed are so deep they could not possibly be said in any other way. For some, clear and concise writing signals the work of a lesser mind that entertains simpler ideas. Complex thought does require a more protracted and involved syntactical structure, but the overall message must still be readable.

Not to be outdone, lawyers closely follow academics in overrating their writing skills. And like academics, they are quick to acknowledge the writing problems of their peers. They say things like: "Most lawyers [not me, mind you] don't write that well. I see so many poorly organized documents [none of which are anything like what I write]. As a profession, we need to do a better job of writing [I'm still not talking about me]."

Although academics and attorneys would top the rankings in any national poll of authorial self-esteem, they do not run away with the title. Most of us misjudge our writing abilities. And it is not because we are all delusional or egomaniacal.

When we write, we regularly omit many of the sense-making connectives—background information, vital explanation, helpful transitions, and supportive logic—vital to creating a text that makes us sound rational. Instead, we "subvocalize" (mentally fill in) these missing links as we write and review our text. Our writing thus makes total sense to us, and usually only to us, because we read it the way no one else does.

To know what it is like to be your reader, take a sample of your best writing and set it aside for several months, long enough to forget the sense-making connectives that swirled in your head at the time you wrote it, but which never made the page. Without the benefit of this additional, unwritten text to guide you, now reread what you wrote. Experiencing your writing this way, in much the same way as would your audience, is eye opening and humbling. Yes, it is easy to overestimate the quality of your writing. Your formerly eloquent words probably do not seem quite as refined as you first thought.

Unfortunately, setting aside a writing assignment for months before returning to its editing is not usually practical, especially if you hope to graduate. Chapter 8, however, does offer a helpful way to immediately gauge the readability of your writing.

Most People Think They Can Develop Strong Writing Skills with Less Effort and Time Than Necessary

Nearly all of us acknowledge the importance of writing well, although we do not always recognize the full extent to which it benefits careers, and nearly everyone will say that writing takes time and effort. But most of us still underestimate just how much time and effort are required. While some writers can compose quickly and elegantly, the process proves labor intensive, particularly for conscientious writers trying to meet their own threshold of excellence. The superb writing they seek is hallmarked by two characteristics:

- It exudes a distinct sound, an unmistakable rhythm and elegance. The writer embraces metaphor and commands a polished syntax that flows so smoothly one can read it aloud without ever stumbling because of awkward phrasing. It is the kind of writing found in such magazines as *The New Yorker, Esquire, The Atlantic, Vanity Fair,* and *Rolling Stone.*
- It also exhibits impeccable structure, which, next to rhythm and elegance, may well be the toughest element of writing to master. A text rich in content can be notably difficult to structure into a unified and coherent whole, where similar ideas come together logically and seamlessly. Even exceptional writers struggle with organization, their eloquence suffering when it is subverted by maverick sentences allowed to roam about untethered to clear, main ideas or main arguments. Orchestrating an orderly, soundly sequenced progression of thoughts is never easy.

Superb writing skills can take a lifetime to develop, and, still, many will never achieve the goal. Thankfully, most writing required by work, school, and home needs to be "only" clear, concise, and compelling. That is where *Renovating Your Writing* comes in.

Unlike beginning composition books that are organized *top-down* (usually starting with how to choose a topic and develop a thesis before moving on to sentence structure and word choice), *Renovating Your Writing* is organized *ground-up,* starting with how to revise words and sentences before taking on how to write paragraphs and pages. This approach reflects the view that rewriting skills are best learned by first understanding the basic units of writing and then building upon them.

Part I, "Strategies, Tactics, and Tips," shows how to efficiently streamline your writing by eliminating unnecessary and distracting verbiage; illustrates how to create an accessible and credible sentence style; details ways you can redesign your paragraph and page structure for maximum impact; and explains how to create unified, coherent paragraphs that strategically carry forth your message.

Part II, "Additional Tools," includes a primer on punctuation, guidelines for writing e-mails, a simple way of determining the readability of your writing, and a unique approach for developing a more cogent style.

Let's begin.

RENO TIP 1.1

RENOVATION TIP

It helps to "rest" your writing. The next time you finish an important assignment, consider it *almost* done. Put it down, walk away, and work on something else for a while. Then return to the assignment and read it as if you are seeing it for the first time; pretend you are the reader. This will allow you to spot the little cracks that cause your reader to stumble, as well as the larger ruptures that level entire understanding. Although you can catch many problems by reading over your message carefully, it becomes more difficult to see all the flaws as you get closer to your writing. Conversely, the longer your writing "rests" between rewritings, the easier it is to pretend you are the reader.

2 Streamlining Your Writing

You can streamline your writing by using smaller words, composing shorter sentences, and eliminating wordiness. Why is it important to pay attention to these matters when more global issues—like developing, structuring, and supporting a thesis—lurk around the bend? Isn't it trivial to discuss word choice, for example, in the context of seemingly more substantive tasks you must complete to create a well-written paper?

Attention and commitment to detail is important because it is the starting point for approaching every aspect of your writing carefully and thoroughly. More than just a step you carry out in the post-production process of your writing, attention and commitment to detail mirrors a perspective that informs all your critical thinking and expression. This concept is underscored throughout the pages that follow, which often allude to the writer's need to make fine distinctions to ensure clear, concise, and compelling expression.

It is easier to see what a sentence is actually saying, what it needs to say, and where it fits in the paragraph—or if it fits at all—when you streamline its content and expose its core. Revising clunky passages by trimming long words, shortening sentence length, and slashing verbosity reveals the essence of your thought. Stripped of all distracting elements, a sentence's meaning and function become more transparent.

ADOPT THE RUNT OF THE (WORD) LITTER

Shorter words, the runts, allow your writing to be read swiftly. Longer words, by contrast, tax and slow the reader. They become like hiccups, each momentarily stopping the reader and leading to a reading experience denser than the sum of its parts. Scraping *unneeded* longer words helps streamline your writing.

This does not mean you should avoid using longer words. You need both short words (two syllables or less) and long ones (three syllables or more) to write clearly, concisely, and compellingly. If the longer word better expresses your meaning in a way no other word will quite do, use it. But if the shorter, more familiar word does the job equally as well, choose it instead.

When you use longer words mainly out of habit or just to sound intelligent, you are limiting the effectiveness of your communication. Always ask yourself, Why am I using the longer word? Do I really need it to express my meaning? If you cannot justify the longer word semantically, opt for its shorter version. If, for example, you want to convey a slight change, the better word is *modification* (five syllables) because it is more precise. But to use *modification* when you mean a full-fledged change is both long winded and misleading. The same can be said if you write *accumulate* (four syllables) instead of *gather* to reference an activity that is immediate rather than long term, or when you choose *demonstrate*, not *show*, to describe a simple, non-illustrative act. In these cases, the longer word is not only space wasting but also incorrect.

Once you begin to rethink your use of long words, you will find that many can be replaced with shorter synonyms without much sacrifice in meaning and that many more long words are not needed. You will find that it is just as easy to *end* the habit as it is to *initiate appropriate dismissal action relative to* the habit.

Take this simple idea made obtuse by using 15 unnecessary long words:

> ORIGINAL   In our **endeavor** to **determine** whether the **proposal** we have **formulated** for a nudist colony in downtown Santa Barbara is **fundamentally** sound, we **anticipate** **engaging** the services of a market research **organization** to **ascertain** whether our **conceptualization** of the market can be **substantiated** by **information accumulated** by **empirical, scientific** research.

Such unnecessary use of long words is common. In the revision, the author employs only two long words (*determine* and *proposal*), while still conveying the essential meaning of the original passage.

> REVISION A   To determine if our proposal for a nudist colony in downtown Santa Barbara is sound, we will hire a research firm to test our view of the market.

Here is another, slightly different version:

> REVISION B   To assess the soundness of our market view that informs our proposal for a nudist colony in downtown Santa Barbara, we will hire a research firm to test our assumptions.

Even the opening page of a manual on, of all things, report writing can miss the mark. The author probably intended to write a *Foreword*, but *Forward* seems more appropriate given the reader may need some kind of military command to get through the text. Nearly 40% of the words are polysyllabic.

> FORWARD
>
> The **various activities** of the **technical personnel** of the Research and **Development Department** have the common **objective** of **acquiring** knowledge and making **profitable application** of this knowledge within

the **company's** sphere of **operations.** The **mechanics** of **successfully achieving** this **objective** include the **inception** of ideas; their **experimental** trial; the **evaluation** of **experimental** results; and, where **economically attractive**, the **adaptation** of **resultant developments** to practice.

Who, other than the author's mom, would want to read this? A better version might say:

FOREWORD

The Research and Development Department seeks knowledge that the company can use profitably. The steps toward this goal include initiating ideas, testing them experimentally, evaluating results, and developing those that show promise of making a profit.

You may yearn for a longer word now and then just to vary your style. After writing *aim* and *goal* several times, you might covet an *objective* or two. Just as longer synonyms are sometimes needed to avoid tiresome repetition, a phrase can replace the monotony of a shorter word. *But* is concise; *on the other hand*, do you want to say it all the time? And should a long word save you three or four short words, use it—if you think your audience knows its meaning.

Your preference, though, should be to select the shorter word first. Frequently, writers say they use words like *endeavor, terminate,* and *utilize* in relief of *try, end,* and *use.* But a look at their writing shows they choose longer words repeatedly before using the shorter versions, if at all.

Purists will argue there is no such thing as a synonym because no two words mean exactly the same. But that should not be taken as license to use longer words indiscriminately. Unless your text requires exceptional precision owing to the nature of the topic and the audience addressed, synonyms will suffice for most writing assignments. To select the right synonym, however, you must have an excellent working vocabulary that includes an assortment of short and long words, enabling you to vary your style without sacrificing readability.

Box 2.1 lists just a few examples of longer words often overused. Next to each is a shorter, simpler word that can usually serve as a good substitute. Some of the words have more than one meaning, allowing for more than one synonym.

BOX 2.1

accentuate. highlight
admonition . . . . warning
aggregate . . . . total
ameliorate. improve
appellation . . . . name
component . . . . part
corroborate . . . . confirm
discontinue . . . . stop

effectuate	effect
elucidate	clarify
endeavor	try
erroneous	wrong
expenditure	expense
illumination	light
indebtedness	debt
innocuous	harmless
locality	place
multiplicity	many
notification	notice
notwithstanding	despite
numerate	count
optimum	best
preeminent	top
prognosticate	predict
remunerate	pay
salutation	greeting
substantiate	prove
trepidation	fear
utilize	use

RATION LONG SENTENCES

Another way of streamlining your writing is by rationing long sentences. A sentence becomes *unnecessarily* long when it contains more than one main thought or when it is so overloaded with extra words that it confuses the reader. No one wants to spend time maneuvering through the maze of a marathon sentence. For easy, interesting reading, sentences should vary in structure and length, but they should never be longer than necessary.

As seen in the previous section, shorter words produce shorter sentences. But the overuse of bigger words is not the only cause of long sentences. In *The Elements of Style*, William Strunk and E. B. White observe: "When you become hopelessly mired in a sentence, it is best to start fresh; do not try to fight your way through against the terrible odds of syntax. Usually what is wrong is that the construction has become too involved at some point; the sentence needs to be broken apart and replaced by two or more shorter sentences." Sometimes all you need to do is add periods to break the endless sentence, as in this example:

ORIGINAL   I was told by a lot of my friends that Professor Stern, also known as The Writing Czar, subtracted points for every grammar, punctuation, usage, and spelling mistake, but I didn't think she would deduct so many points from my paper that I would get a negative score on my first college assignment and end up with the lowest grade in the class, all of which may help explain why I handed in my less-than-great paper even though I knew it wasn't great by any means it still seemed good enough to probably get at least a C, so that's why I'm now concerned and think I should change direction and not major in English.

REVISION   I was told by a lot of my friends that Professor Stern, also known as The Writing Czar, subtracted points for every grammar, punctuation, usage, and spelling mistake. But I didn't think she would deduct so many points from my paper that I would get a negative score on my first college assignment and end up with the lowest grade in the class. All of which may help explain why I handed in my less-than-great paper. Even though I knew it wasn't great by any means, it still seemed good enough to probably get at least a C. So that's why I'm now concerned and think I should change direction and not major in English.

More editing, however, is usually required of long, unreadable sentences.

ORIGINAL   Assuming that Mark and Marla are able to convince the city council, which includes three members who are vegetarians and active in the cause, to commercially rezone the property on which they would like to build their restaurant, The Lion Fillet, and assuming Mark and Marla are also able to persuade potential customers to their restaurant that the eating of exotic game food is healthy, as well as nutritious, not to mention all-American, and, finally, assuming that Mark and Marla can guarantee both timely and consistent delivery of game food products from their African and American distributors, their new restaurant should be successful.

Huh? In this runaway sentence, the writer's thoughts gallop along unharnessed for 103 words. The sentence's conclusion ("their new restaurant should be successful") is nearly lost by the time readers finally reach the end. Breaking this sentence into shorter ones, labeled and numbered, would allow the writer to emphasize the main ideas and to rebuild them around a conclusion that comes first.

REVISION A   For their new restaurant, The Lion Fillet, to succeed, Mark and Marla must do three things: (1) They must convince the city council, which includes three vegetarian activists, to rezone the proposed restaurant site to commercial property. (2) They must show potential customers that eating exotic game is healthy, nutritious, and all-American. (3) They must ensure timely and consistent meat deliveries from their African and American distributors.

Or, instead, the writer could use bullets to highlight the key points of the message.

REVISION B   For their new restaurant, The Lion Fillet, to succeed, Mark and Marla must do three things:
- convince the city council, which includes three vegetarian activists, to rezone the proposed restaurant site to commercial property;
- show potential customers that eating exotic game is healthy, nutritious, and all-American; and
- ensure timely and consistent meat deliveries from their African and American distributors.

Longer sentences also come about when writers choose scrawny words that require the help of adjectives and adverbs. When these adjectives and adverbs, in turn, are insufficient and need their own additional modification, the problem escalates. Some modifying words, such as *very*, function as little more than the writer's concession of having initially chosen anemic language, a problem *very* will not remedy. Mark Twain famously advised, "Substitute 'damn' every time you're inclined to write 'very'; your editor will delete it and the writing will be just as it should be."

Richard Weaver, in *The Ethics of Rhetoric*, argues that the excess use of adjectives and adverbs signifies a lesser writer.

The adjective is . . . a word of secondary status and force. Its burden is an attribute, or something added. In the order of being to which reference has been made, the noun can exist without the adjective, but not the adjective without the noun. . . . The adjective is question-begging; that is to say, if the thing to be expressed is real, it will be expressed through a substantive [a word or group of words that function as a noun]; if it is expressed mainly through adjectives, there is something defective in its reality, since it has gone for secondary support.

Weaver concedes there are "situations in which such modifiers do make a useful contribution, but as a general rule . . . a style is stronger when it depends mainly upon substantives sharp enough to convey their own attributes." The same, he says, holds true for the adverb.

The effects of text messaging and tweeting on the development of writing skills may go well beyond the widespread complaint that they spur poor writing habits because of the vernacular they spawn and the colloquial style they invite. On one hand, the physical constraints of texting and tweeting on a small keyboard lead to a verb-oriented, active-voice style where writers shy away from all but the most necessary adjectives and adverbs. The medium rewards easy-to-read sentences that get to the point quickly. On the other hand, texting and tweeting also encourage a short-sentence-only prose preoccupied with surfaces—reportage as opposed to analysis and exploration. Insofar as language and thought are inseparable (our thinking influences our language; our language influences our thinking), writing exclusively in short sentences may promote a simple, uncomplicated view of the world, where elements are seen as discrete from and unaffecting of one another.

Still, the short sentence is championed, frequently with cult-like admiration. Some writers want to break up every long sentence, however competently written, just because of length. The result is to burden the reader with the task of having to mentally connect two or more parts of a logical whole. The problem of sentence slicing taken to the extreme can be seen in this example:

ORIGINAL	My dog has three legs. She weighs 250 pounds. She is blind in one eye. She is missing both her ears. She runs a quarter mile in under 30 seconds.
REVISION	Although my dog has three legs, weighs 250 pounds, suffers blindness in one eye, and is missing both her ears, she still manages to run a quarter mile in under 30 seconds.

Which version best communicates the *single* thought that your challenged dog is one fast Chihuahua? And lest we forget the big dogs, which of the following versions more efficiently connects the conclusion with the supporting rationale?

ORIGINAL	Great Danes are smart. They are affectionate. They are loyal. For these reasons I love the big fellas.
REVISION	I love Great Danes because they are smart, affectionate, and loyal.

In the revision, four short sentences (18 words total) are combined into one (still short) sentence of 11 words that better serves the writer's purpose. A sentence should not be broken into multiple sentences unless you intend to express multiple thoughts.

Using short sentences exclusively can also produce a choppy, childlike-sounding effect that can be distracting. Varying your sentence lengths avoids the problem of having your writing come across like a third-grade textbook.

Clearly, it is unwise to banish longer sentences from your writing. Save them to express more complex thought. Academic writing, in particular, often mandates the type of detailed explanation and qualification that increases sentence length. Long sentences are not a problem if they convey what short sentences cannot. The good news is that you can create readable sentences of any length if you write well and know the rules of punctuation, which are discussed in Chapter 6.

In sum, it makes good sense to vary your sentence length. A style laden with long sentences, no matter how concise and elegant, challenges the reader's processing skills, whereas one that relies only on short sentences can seem halting and simplistic. A mixture of short and long sentences makes for a more engaging reading experience.

So, too, does varying your sentence structure. Aside from being dull and dreary, repetitive sentence patterns call attention to themselves, misdirecting the reader's focus away from more important concerns. In *The Technique of Clear Writing*, Robert Gunning, one of the pioneers of the clear writing movement that began in America in the mid-1900s, offers several examples of the different ways of saying, "Clear, interesting writing contains all sorts of variety" (Box 2.2).

BOX 2.2

PERSONAL	Variety will give your writing clarity and interest.
CONDITIONAL	If you would employ variety, you would write more interestingly.
SPECIFIC	Variety in words, sentences, tones, and structure is a key to interesting writing.
NEGATIVE	Writing that has no variety lacks sparkle and interest.
COMPARISON	Writing that has variety interests the reader; prose that lacks it is dull.
PREPOSITIONAL BEGINNING	Without variety, prose is dull.
PARTICIPIAL	Lacking variety, prose is uninteresting.
IMPERATIVE	Put variety in what you write in order to interest your reader.

Many writers tend to structure all their sentences the same way: They begin with the subject followed by the predicate. *I* [subject] *appreciate a graceful sentence* [predicate]. The subject, expressed by a noun or pronoun, is the who or what around which the key action in the sentence revolves. The predicate, which describes the key action in the sentence (which can sometimes be more like a condition), is a verb that may also include (1) an object (the direct or indirect recipient of the action), or (2) a complement (one or more words that rename or describe either the object or the subject), or (3) both. For example: *I* [subject] *appreciate* [verb] *a graceful sentence* [object]. *This paragraph* [subject] *is* [verb] *boring* [subject complement]. *Poorly written sentences* [subject] *make* [verb] *me* [object] *sad* [object complement].

Overuse of the subject–predicate formula becomes stale quickly. To vary your sentence structure, think of how you might write your typical subject–predicate sentence in a less standard way without it sounding odd. Rather than *I enjoy reading a graceful sentence,* consider alternatives, such as the following:

> *Reading a graceful sentence* [subject] *brings me great enjoyment* [predicate].

> *One of my greatest enjoyments* [subject] *is reading a graceful sentence* [predicate].

Breaking the tedium of repetitive sentence structure is not difficult. Words can be moved about in various ways to freshen your style and to emphasize one thought over another. Once you see the need for variation, you will have no problem finding all kinds of new ways to write old sentences. You might even pose a rhetorical question (a dramatic question to which everyone knows the answer) to drive home your idea or argument. *After all, wouldn't you want to use every possible tool to enhance your persuasability? And would any reader ever object to a sentence style that is richer and more varied?*

WRITE ~~VERY~~ TIGHTLY ~~WITHOUT VERBOSITY~~

Although we speak of them in the same breath, clarity and conciseness are not always complementary. Usually, the more concisely you write, the clearer your message. But if you exclude vital facts to achieve conciseness, your clarity will suffer, and so will your conciseness if you keep restating content for the sake of clarity.

Conciseness is not a matter of just writing shorter sentences. A sentence of 30, 40, or even 50 words is concise if its main thought cannot effectively be conveyed in fewer words. And a sentence of nine or ten words is way too long if it can be said as well in five or six words. Conciseness means using the fewest words necessary, regardless of the number, to express yourself cogently.

You can avoid wordiness by scrutinizing your writing to make sure every word pulls its weight. Even when drafting an e-mail, you can get into the habit of shaving needless words. The trick is to cut the fat, not the muscle. Express your ideas or arguments and the evidence and reasoning that support them as concisely as possible without compromising their integrity for the sake of brevity. Your challenge is to craft messages that are simple, but not simplistic.

It is not unusual for a message to be both wordy and incomplete: The writer presents a verbose conclusion—*I am of the opinion that it would be beneficial to achieve an expansion of student enrollment in all our remedial courses*—and then does not support it with any evidence and reasoning. Conciseness does not equal the absence of proof. An incomplete message is hardly persuasive.

The first step in purging any message of its wordiness is not to look for whole paragraphs or pages to cut, but to make sure your every word is needed. Even a short text can be twice as long as necessary.

ORIGINAL   This is to inform you that we have your order dated March 16 for four dozen gold Spy Pens with Disappearing Ink, for which we want to express our thanks.

We regret to advise you that we are no longer making this pen in gold and hereby wish to advise that we are currently producing it only in black. However, we do have a gold-colored Advanced Spy Pen with Disappearing Ink, which includes a self-destruction switch. The Advanced Spy Pen with Disappearing Ink and self-destruction switch costs an extra $9.95 per unit. Please indicate whether you wish us to ship you four dozen black Spy Pens with Disappearing Ink or four dozen gold Advanced Spy Pens with Disappearing ink and self-destruction switch.

Awaiting your favorable advice, I remain . . .

REVISION   Thank you for your March 16 order for four dozen gold Spy Pens with Disappearing Ink.

We now make this pen in black only. However, our Advanced Spy Pen with Disappearing Ink, which also

> includes a self-destruction switch, comes in gold. It costs an extra $9.95 per pen. Would you like us to fill your order with black Spy Pens or gold Advanced Spy Pens?

In the revision, 65 words do the work of the 128 in the original. The writer's points are introduced faster, and the closing question, unlike the original's weak ending, invites action. Eliminating wordiness increases the chance your audience will read, understand, and act upon your message.

Pleonasm, the use of more words than necessary, afflicts much of today's writing. Pleonastic examples are so familiar we seldom stop to consider what they really mean. When we do, we realize how little they say. Note the variations of this familiar opening:

> We would like to talk with you . . . on the matter of
> in connection with
> in reference to
> in relation to
> on the subject of
> with regard to
> with respect to . . . our new cell
> phone offers.

One word, *about*, could replace any of the prepositional phrases used here, resulting in a tighter opening sentence.

"Clutter," says William Zinsser, in *On Writing Well*, "is the disease of American writing. We are a society strangling in unnecessary words, circular constructions, pompous frills and meaningless jargon." Such writing comes about in part because we want to sound intelligent and professional. Self-conscious about how we project, we embrace an artificial, lofty-aspiring style where needless complexity rules the page. We equate pretentious tone with sophistication, unnatural formality with elegance, meandering sentences with profoundness. Focusing more on ourselves than on our readers, we produce the sort of wordy, affected writing we would never dream of speaking. *We need to increase the size of the parking lot* becomes *The parking lot where we currently domicile our personal vehicular transportation should undergo structural augmentation*. Descartes said, "I think, therefore I am." The word hoarder says, "I engage in cognitive processing that functions ultimately to substantiate my real-world existence." Shakespeare said, "A coward dies a thousand deaths, but the valiant taste death but once." The word hoarder says, "Those having a character of timidity will metaphorically experience extinction often, whereas those having a character of courage will literally experience extinction once."

Most of the stilted wordiness plaguing so much writing is actually learned. The text swelling starts as soon as you get that first of many school writing assignments having a minimum word requirement: "Papers must be at least 1,500 words." You begin, *This essay describes the political system of the United Kingdom*. And then you count: 10 words; 1,490 to go. I'm never going to finish. Ok, let me try stretching it a bit. *This essay has chosen a very important subject area that is worthy of study, which is consequently the reason why it was selected as the topic for this term paper. The country that is known as the United Kingdom will be discussed in terms of its political system in the pages that follow.* You count again: 53 words—now that's more like it; only 1,447 to go!

Later, when you enter the workforce, you learn to become still wordier, this time spurred by the corporate sense of what sounds business-like. *We received your complaint today and will investigate the matter* is edited by your first supervisor to read, *Your complaint has been officially received and recorded, as of today, and will be investigated further by our staff in an appropriate manner.* Meanwhile, down the hallway in another meeting, upper management is complaining about the problems of poor employee writing.

RENO TIP **2.1**

RENOVATION TIP

Minimum word requirements discourage conciseness because they reward the writer for adding more text. Instead, imagine having to stay within a maximum word limit. Take any assignment you must complete that does not have a required minimum word or page length and estimate its likely length given your experience with similar assignments. Cut your estimate by one-third and use this figure as your limit for the assignment. Forced to write concisely, you will be surprised by the results.

The easiest editing is when you can delete extra words (the bolded portions in the following examples) without having to add or change other words in the sentence.

- **In order** to finish **the completion of** my book on the history of the question mark, I wrote **all** throughout **the months of** July and August.
- We should eliminate **the occurrence of** wordiness now, not by **the** early **part of** next month!
- The **issue in** question is whether she would have been elected Homecoming Queen prior to **the start of** her learning to write concisely.
- **It is** often **the case that** good writers are also good lovers.
- **A woman named** Natalie, who has a Ph.D. in **the field of** English, told me so.

A single word can frequently replace several others without changing the sentence's meaning.

- We hold conciseness seminars **on a monthly basis** [monthly], but we would like to hold them **on a weekly basis** [weekly].
- This is a check **in the amount of** [for] $50 to cover the bet I lost on apostrophes.

Or
This $50 check covers the bet I lost on apostrophes.

- We could not complete the project on time **due to the fact that** [because] our editor was arrested for stealing composition books.
- Your argument **is based on the assumption** [assumes] the famous self-help author lied about having 47 assistants.
- Iris eyed the report **for the purpose of** [to] **examining** [examine] the facts.
- **In light of the fact that** [Because] Sue cannot write a lick, she should be fired.
  Or
  Sue should be fired because she cannot write a lick.
  Or
  Sue cannot write a lick and should be fired.
- He performed best **in any situation in which he was** [when] asked to revise quickly and secretly.
- My editorial responsibilities were always **in a state of change** [changing] **in the course of** [during] my career at Evolving Industries.
- I **am of the thought that** [think] your **use of** syntax is breathtaking.

  That can usually be deleted if its absence does not create an awkward-sounding or confusing sentence. *I told Buddy the bear* [as in Smokey the Bear?] *was eating our writing journals. It was the lion Buddy* [another animal named Buddy?] *was trying to avoid. I believe the lion* [because the lion has credibility?] *was friendlier before we named him.*

- **Any number of** [many, some] rejected writers believe that the best books never get published.

  This is an unusual case where the sentence is both wordy and inconcise. How many is "any number of"?

- **During the time of my stay** [while] at MIT, I studied the writing habits of wrestling coaches **all over the world** [worldwide].

  You could also say *At MIT,* but the meaning would be slightly different. *While at MIT* suggests you went to MIT primarily to study something other than the writing habits of wrestling coaches, *At MIT* implies you went specifically to MIT to study their writing habits.

Sometimes a simple change in punctuation allows you to delete words and collapse two or more sentences into one that is shorter and better.

ORIGINAL	I have five favorite punctuation marks. They are commas, semicolons, colons, dashes, and ellipses.
REVISION	I have five favorite punctuation marks: commas, semicolons, colons, dashes, and ellipses.
ORIGINAL	My book on the history of the question mark will appeal to two groups. One group would be people who love punctuation. The other group would be people with a lot of time on their hands.

REVISION	My book on the history of the question mark will appeal to two groups: people who love punctuation and people with a lot of time on their hands.
ORIGINAL	I love to read novels. Another one of my loves is poetry, and I also love literary nonfiction.
REVISION	I love to read novels, poetry, and literary nonfiction.
ORIGINAL	My footnoting skills include knowledge of all major style guides. I learned these skills when I was on academic probation.
REVISION	My footnoting skills, learned when I was on academic probation, include knowledge of all major style guides.

The preceding sampling of wordy sentences illustrates how even the shortest of content can be inconcise. Lengthier sentences, a staple of academic writing, can usually be streamlined even more.

ORIGINAL	Although there are numerous cases of the writer's lack of critical thinking skills that abound, the purpose of this paper is to focus on three of those specific examples in question, each one representing a very completely different aspect of the problem. (42 words)
REVISION	Although numerous cases of the writer's lack of critical thinking skills abound, this paper focuses on three examples, each representing a different aspect of the problem. (26 words)
ORIGINAL	The accuracy and veracity of the writer's authored personality pieces were rarely ever challenged by the individuals the writer depicted, primarily because many of the people with whom the writer had interacted, and subsequently depicted, had no interest in providing corrective responses or were not in a position to have the means to provide corrective responses to the author's writings. (60 words)
REVISION	The accuracy of the writer's personality pieces was rarely challenged by the individuals depicted, many of whom had neither the interest nor the means to provide corrective responses. (28 words)
ORIGINAL	Satirical oxymorons have as their function the expression of political and social viewpoints through the referring of their targeted subject, the one meant to be satirized, as "oxymoronic"—for example, *military intelligence, civil engineer, Microsoft Works*—or by the coupling of their targeted subject with a word that is usually viewed to be a positive descriptor and then referring back to the construction created as "oxymoronic," as seen in such examples as *honest* politician, *compassionate* IRS agent, or *smart* reality show star. (82 words)

REVISION   Satirical oxymorons express political and social viewpoints by referring to their targeted subject as "oxymoronic"—for example, *military intelligence, civil engineer, Microsoft Works*—or by coupling their targeted subject with a positive descriptor and then labeling the term "oxymoronic," as in *honest* politician, *compassionate* IRS agent, or *smart* reality show star. (51 words)

Once your consciousness is raised and you become sensitized to the siren of verbal excess and the many ways that "habit phrases" fatten your writing, you can quickly spot the problems and self-correct them.

Box 2.3 lists more examples of the scores of phrases that squander your reader's time. Next to each is one word, sometimes two, that says nearly the same thing.

BOX 2.3

a large number of	many, most
all of a sudden	suddenly
as a matter of fact	in fact
as of late	lately
at a future date	later
at the present time	now
at this juncture	now
enclosed herewith	enclosed
despite the fact that	although
has the implication	implies
in a timely manner	timely
in order that	so
in recognition of this fact	hence, thus
in the event that	if
is able to	can
is an example of	exemplifies
is an illustration of	illustrates
is responsible for choosing	chooses
it is apparent that	apparently
it would seem that	seemingly
make it possible	enable
make provisions for	provide
negate the possibility of	preclude

notwithstanding the fact that . . . . . . although, despite
on a continual basis . . . . continually
on the decrease . . . . decreasing
on the grounds that . . . . because
provided that . . . . if
read through . . . . read
somewhere in the neighborhood of . . . around
the ability to . . . . can
we are of the opinion . . . . we think

Occasionally, the wordier version is preferable to its shorter counterpart. It is more concise to say *disabled person* than *a person with a disability*, but the positioning of *disabled* as an adjective in *disabled person* highlights the disability and serves to define the person. A *person with a disability* is wordier, but it emphasizes the person over the disability and demotes *disability* to a secondary role by relegating it to a prepositional phrase (i.e., *with a disability*).

Most wordiness can be eliminated by "blue-penciling" (line-by-line editing) your text. Sometimes, though, only a new draft will do. If you find yourself rereading a windy passage and not knowing where to begin editing, it is probably time to start from scratch. The windy passage is likely to be much longer than necessary.

ORIGINAL	I am eager to solicit any and all editing recommendations that you may wish to make, and you can be assured that each and every such recommendation will be given my utmost, careful review. (34 words)
REVISION	I welcome your editing suggestions, which I will review carefully. (10 words)
ORIGINAL	We wish to advise you that we have thoroughly and completely examined your July travel expense transactions request form, and that we have decided to make an affirmative recommendation regarding your request for reimbursement. Your claim for $7 travel reimbursement has been granted. Enclosed is a check for that amount. (50 words)
REVISION	We approved your claim for travel reimbursement. Enclosed is a check for $7. (13 words)
ORIGINAL	If we continue to defer maintenance operations through our failure to supply sufficient funds to make needed repairs as they naturally become necessary from time to time, the operating efficiency of the Mash Pit Arena will steadily diminish to the point that the situation will be

able to be corrected only by our undertaking of a major construction project. (59 words)

REVISION   If we continually fail to repair the Mash Pit Arena when the need arises, the problems will worsen and eventually cost more to fix. (24 words)

What about contractions? Especially in informal writing, contractions create a natural, conversational tone. And they consume less space by turning two words into one. Uncontracted forms, however, can emphasize ideas more effectively. Greater warning, for example, is conveyed by *You should not* than *You shouldn't*. The longer form, *not*, also allows for additional emphasis, such as *not*, **not**, NOT (small capitals), or NOT. *We will decide* is stronger than *We'll decide*.

Generally, contractions should be avoided in formal documents. When convention calls for a more elevated style, contractions, abbreviations, colloquialisms, and exclamation marks will seem out of place. In *Fumblerules*, William Safire writes: "You don't wear a tie to a ballgame, and you do not wear loafers to a church wedding. In the same way, you shouldn't use formal English when your intent is to be sassy and breezy, nor should you employ contractions in a solemn speech or formal letter."

Perhaps the greater value of contractions is that they induce readable writing. Edward Bailey, in *The Plain English Approach to Business Writing*, observes that using contractions improves your "write-ability" because they prompt a conversational style that leads to shorter, simpler, more direct sentences. The same writer who would say *Don't do it* will also adopt, unconsciously, the stiffer, longer style that the uncontracted form seemingly engages: *Do not participate in such activities at this time.* Bailey suggests writing everything first with contractions to ensure readability, after which formal documents can be "*un*contracted."

RENO TIP **2.2**

RENOVATION TIP

When you first set out to ruthlessly delete unneeded words, your sentences may start to sound choppy. Adding words such as *also, accordingly, additionally, consequently, furthermore, moreover, hence, so, therefore, thus,* and *too* can help you transition between thoughts more smoothly. As your writing improves and your structure and style become more fluid, you will find less need for these "connectors" because your sentences will follow one another naturally.

Chapter 2

EXERCISES

EXERCISE 1. For each word, come up with at least one shorter synonym of two syllables or less.

additional . . . .

altercation . . . .

anticipate . . . .

approximately . . . .

assistance . . . .

commitment. . . . .

compensate . . . .

culminate . . . .

encounter . . . .

equivalent . . . .

fundamental . . . .

maintenance. . . . .

necessitate . . . .

proficiency . . . .

recollection . . . .

subsequent . . . .

sufficient. . . . .

terminate . . . .

EXERCISE 2. Streamline the following sentence, a 79-word monstrosity, by de-bloating it and breaking it into two or more cogent sentences; be sure your rewrite includes all the key points in the original sentence.

In accordance with the director's recent authorization to formalize arrangements with Dr. Renovation, who will be conducting a series of workshops for us with the purpose of simplifying, clarifying, and making more readable those written materials integral to the effective functioning of the company, the director requests that samples of all written materials, typical of those prepared by each manager, be forwarded to the director by Monday in order that they can be given to Dr. Renovation for commentary.

EXERCISE 3. Revise each wordy phrase down to one word.

at an early date . . . .

for the reason that . . . .

has the ability to . . . .

in large measure . . . .

in the near future . . . .

in the vicinity of . . . .

is a representation of . . . .

is an indication of. . . . .

is based on the inference. . . . .

it is evident that. . . . .

it is probable that . . . .

most of the time. . . . .

offers the suggestion . . . .

on a regular basis . . . .

on the increase . . . .

performs the function of . . . .

take the place of . . . .

to a large degree . . . .

EXERCISE 4. Your mission, should you choose to accept: restore these famous words from the worlds of film and television back to their original eloquence.

A. I am unequivocally directing you to immediately demonstrate your capacity to monetarily enrich me.

B. I will extend a proposal to the individual in question, the terms of which are of such an attractive nature that the chances of his rendering a rejection of the offer are not likely.

C. I guarantee with utmost certainty my revisitation of body and mind upon the situation in which we currently find ourselves.

D. Are you offering what should be viewed as your preliminary response regarding your position on the question, or are you presenting a more definitive conclusion that represents the finality of your thinking.

E. Apparently, you are under the impression that you can engage in terpsichorean activity with success.

EXERCISE 5. Write a complete short story, with a beginning, a middle, and an end, using a maximum of 55 words. Your story must have a setting, one or more characters (you could be one of the characters), and some kind of conflict that gets resolved at the end. For a discussion of how the process of authoring 55-word short stories promotes cogent writing, see Chapter 9.

3 Constructing Sentences

GET TO THE POINT, *TODAY*

As shown in Chapter 2, using smaller words, relying on shorter sentences, and eliminating wordiness will enable you to write sentences that get to your point quickly. Additionally, it will help to rid your sentences of windy prefaces. Most long windups state the obvious.

- **After a thorough and careful review and consideration of the facts** [as if to say you do not normally look closely at the facts], I determined that Sadie, 72, should be promoted to Head Bouncer for these reasons . . .

Or they squander valuable space.

- **In response to your question about whether we provide free legal services to the rich, the answer is** yes, we provide free legal services to the rich.
- **Per your request,** enclosed is a list of websites that caution against creating your own website.
  Or
  Here is a list of websites that caution against creating your own website.

Instead of wasting part of your first sentence referencing your reader's question or request, which is less important than your response, use the subject line in e-mails, memos, and letters to signal the topic you are addressing.

In the next example, the entire first sentence can be deleted and replaced with a short summary phrase, *policy on delinquent debts*, which goes in the subject line. Your message could then begin with what is more important: answering your reader's question about delinquent debts, which you do by leading with the good news.

- **We received your e-mail yesterday inquiring about whether we still break the arms of gamblers who have difficulty paying**

their debts on time. No, we no longer break or sever limbs because of delinquent debts.

After deleting the long windup, you may need to add a few words to get the sentence moving.

- **With the desired, planned objective in mind of improving** [To improve] everyone's writing skills, we tied medical plan benefits to writing proficiencies.
- **As far as our observations are concerned, we found** [We observed] several cases where stronger writers took fewer sick days than weaker writers.

Other slow sentence beginnings, such as starting with *there are*, also weaken the reader's engagement. Deleting *There are . . . who/that . . .* , which you can do most of the time, creates a faster, more powerful sentence. Take this slow mover: ***There are*** *nine people* ***who*** *want to date me. There are . . . who* adds nothing and intrudes upon the sentence's two major elements: *nine people* and *want to date me.* Besides, it is much more likely that the first words out of anyone facing the ecstasy of this predicament would be ***nine*** *people,* not *There are.*

The *There are . . . who/that . . .* construction may come after a dependent clause or a phrase.

- After Sheriff Tuff took over, **there were** fewer cyber-criminals **who** roamed the streets of Computerville.
- In my view, **there are** no rewards **that** justify betraying a gorgeous roommate.

After deleting *There are . . . who/that . . .* , you may find yourself needing to add, change, or rearrange a word or two to make the sentence work.

ORIGINAL	There are few job openings for inexperienced lion tamers.
REVISION	Few job openings exist for inexperienced lion tamers.
ORIGINAL	There is the view held by many murderers that media-portrayed violence is not socially harmful.
REVISION	Many murderers think media-portrayed violence is not socially harmful.
ORIGINAL	There are several brilliant ideas about text messaging that I will text to the Conference on Texting.
REVISION	I will text several brilliant ideas about text messaging to the Conference on Texting.

START WITH ACTIVE ACTORS

In active voice, the sentence's subject **acts.** *I* [subject] *bought* [active verb] *a new robot.* In passive voice, the subject receives the action or is **acted upon.** *A new robot* [subject] *was bought* [passive verb] *by me.* Overuse of passive voice leads to wordy, stilted, listless sentences.

Active voice pervades all our speech, whether it is about business, school, politics, sports, romance, or home life. When people talk to one another, it is natural to start with themselves (the actor) and make themselves the subject of the sentence. They say, *I believe*, not *It is believed by me*. An executive will tell another, *Our company lost money by owning our 325 Hummers instead of leasing them*. But then the executive will write, *It was determined that money was lost through owning, rather than leasing, 325 Hummers*. Such cumbersome prose lacks muscle because it leads with a weak helping verb (was), rather than the more important action (lost).

Active and passive verbs can be any tense.

Active Voice

Present tense:	She manages the Writer's Block Saloon.
Past tense:	She managed the Writer's Block Saloon.
Future tense:	She will manage the Writer's Block Saloon.

Passive Voice

Present tense:	The Writer's Block Saloon is managed by her.
Past tense:	The Writer's Block Saloon was managed by her.
Future tense:	The Writer's Block Saloon will be managed by her.

Active verbs bring writing to life by streamlining sentences and emphasizing action. They also sound more conversational. When your aunt Rita asks whether you received the birthday gift she sent, you respond: *Yeah, I got it. Thanks!* Or should you remember she once taught English, you reply: *Yes, I received it. Thank you!* But you would never say: *Yes, your birthday gift was received by me. You are to be thanked.* Yet it is common to write sentences that are structurally similar: *Your letter was received by us. The issues you raised have been discussed and evaluated by our staff. Our attempt to rectify the situation will be guided by our corporate policy, which is explained below by several more passive voice sentences.* And should this not satisfy your customer, he or she might write back in kind, *It is thought by me that Hell should be gone to by you.*

The verb can be the strongest or the weakest word in a sentence. Active verbs invigorate writing, helping to ensure your sentences are tighter and sharper. Box 3.1 compares sentences in passive versus active voice.

BOX 3.1

Passive	Active
The firm's annual $10,000 award for the best mix of short and long words in a five-page report was won by Max.	Max won the firm's annual $10,000 award for the best mix of long and short words in a five-page report.
A modified payment plan was written by the creditors before they went to jail.	The creditors wrote a modified payment plan before they went to jail.

The decision to strengthen the English Department's Three Strikes Rule on overuse of passive voice was unilaterally made by the dean.	The dean unilaterally decided to strengthen the English Department's Three Strikes Rule on overuse of passive voice.
Our former marketing manager believed that more buying would be engaged in by people during a recession.	Our former marketing manager believed that people would buy more during a recession.
Her pledge never to marry a grammar-challenged man was made by her on her tenth birthday.	On her tenth birthday, she pledged never to marry a grammar-challenged man.
More time and effort have been required by this 20-person project than the initial 30 minutes allotted.	The 20-person project required more time and effort than the initial 30 minutes allotted.
A ten billion dollar accounting error was made. (missing actor)	The student intern made a ten billion dollar accounting error. (actor added)

It is easy to fall into the habit of using passive voice and to become oblivious to the extent of your practice. You unconsciously reel off one passive voice sentence after another.

ORIGINAL   On June 9, **information was requested** by you concerning what **criteria are applied** in determining the company's Most Active Voice Writer of the Month. **Discussion of this matter was engaged in** a few years ago, in 2007. **A criteria statement was issued. The criteria now being followed** are the same as what was in effect in 2007.

You can avoid being stuck in the passive voice zone by continually asking, Who is the actor in the sentence—who is responsible for the action—and is that actor (person or thing) the subject of my sentence? When you ask these questions of the preceding passage, the answers look like this:

REVISION   On June 9, **you asked** how we determine our Most Active Voice Writer of the Month. **The company's managers discussed** this matter a few years ago, in 2007. **They issued** a criteria statement, which is still in effect.

The use of active voice enhances your credibility because it portrays you as confident and forthright. You are not afraid to identify the actor's role in producing the action. You write, *I mistakenly fired my proofreader*, not *My proofreader was mistakenly fired* (actor left out). Active voice engenders a sensibility where actors take direct responsibility for their actions. Not surprisingly, the best corporate mission statements are written in active voice.

The previous sentence, of course, was written in passive voice, just like this one, all of which raises the question, When is it appropriate to use passive voice?

Passive voice is appropriate under the following conditions:

THE ACTOR (THE PERSON OR THING COMMITTING THE ACTION IN THE SENTENCE) IS LESS IMPORTANT THAN THE OBJECT AFFECTED BY THE ACTION.
* The massage parlor was vandalized.
* My pet turkey was stolen.
* I was punched in the face.

Without knowing the actors in these examples, you could still use active voice—*Someone vandalized the massage parlor; Someone stole my pet turkey; Someone punched me in the face*—but you would then be emphasizing the less significant actor over the more significant object of the action. For the last example, you could say, *I received a punch in the face*, in which case you would be speaking in active, but odd, voice.

Sometimes the actor is deemphasized not only because the object of the action is more important but also because the actor is obvious.

* My mail is delivered before 10 AM. (actor: the mailman)
* Barack Obama was elected the 44th president. (actor: the voters)
* My favorite television show, *Writing Problems of the Rich and Famous*, was canceled. (actor: the network)

Other times where you might use passive voice:

YOU WANT TO MINIMIZE THE ACTOR'S RESPONSIBILITY.
* The crucial files were delivered late by Bill, the gun-toting favorite son of our CEO.

YOU WANT TO ELIMINATE THE ACTOR'S RESPONSIBILITY.
* The crucial files were delivered late. As a result, it was decided [by whom?] that we would all work on Christmas Eve to finish the project.

Although the aim of minimizing or eliminating the actor's responsibility is usually to protect the guilty, sometimes the intent is more honorable. In early child-rearing, for example, assigning blame to infants for accidental behavior seems futile. Some experts contend, but not without controversy, it is better to focus on the problem and say, *The milk spilled* (passive voice) than *You spilled the milk* (active voice).

YOU WANT TO SOUND OBJECTIVE AND PROFESSIONAL.
* It is recommended after reviewing input from all sides that Krusher, our boa constrictor mascot, be placed on administrative leave.

The writer wants to emphasize the recommendation over the recommender. Academics and other professionals similarly try to stress the objectivity of their work by often using passive voice to minimize their role as actors in producing their findings.

YOU WANT TO EMPHASIZE THE RELATIONSHIP BETWEEN TWO IDEAS.
* To ensure its financial stability, the company developed a 50-step restructuring plan, which was implemented with great fanfare. That plan would later be blamed for causing the downfall of the company.

The passive-voiced, second sentence structurally aligns the key element, the plan, of both sentences.

YOU WANT TO VARY YOUR STYLE.
- A new corporate sales brochure and pinup calendar were designed and completed by me.

    Because your previous three sentences began with *I*, followed by an accomplishment, this stylistic change-up makes you sound less egotistical. Better ways, however, exist to solve the problem. In a job application letter, for example, you can eliminate *I* by bulleting your duties and successes, which also allows you to start each entry with a positive, action-oriented verb. For example:

As Assistant Bookstore Manager of the campus bookstore, I accomplished the following:
- Designed a new sales brochure and pin-up calendar
- Supervised and trained a staff of 15
- Trained and mentored nine new employees
- Coordinated all strategic sales campaigns
- Managed the budget and approved all allocations

YOU WANT TO BUILD SUSPENSE.
- The best annual report for 2010 was written by [drum roll] Billy Shakespeare.

Writing in passive voice can be a difficult habit to break because it becomes second nature. Word-processing software with grammar-check features, despite not always being accurate, can help bring passive voice constructions to your attention. A good understanding of active and passive voice lets you know whether to accept or reject your software's advice. Most of the time, the best choice will be obvious. Still, you may write a sentence where although there is no compelling reason to use passive voice, it saves words and sounds fine. In Chapter 5, the author went around and around before finally choosing the active voice version of these two sentences:

- They [weak arguments] affect the reader's overall perception of whether the writer is credible and to what extent *anything said should be believed.*
- They [weak arguments] affect the reader's overall perception of whether the writer is credible and to what extent *the reader should believe anything the writer says.*

Which do you prefer?

AVOID VERBY NOUNS

Compounding the problem of passive voice overuse is the related fault of turning active verbs into nouns. Like passive verbs, nominalized verbs (verbs changed into nouns), particularly when positioned at the beginning of sentences, result in wordy constructions that dilute the crux of the expressed action. When you nominalize a sentence's natural verb, you must add another, less important verb to complete the sentence grammatically. Instead of *We will study* [verb] *the problem,* the smotherer writes, *We will undertake* [verb] *a study* [noun] *of the problem.* Or worse: *We will undertake to do a study of the problem.*

Noun endings that alert you to smothered verbs include *-ion, -tion, -ing, -ment, -ant, -ent, -ance,* and *-able.* In Box 3.2, compare the hypothetical newspaper story on the left to the one on the right.

BOX 3.2

Smothered Verbs	Action Verbs
Hazyl Dempsey, executive director, called public atten**tion** today to the recent resump**tion** of opera**tions** by the Good Ferret Protectors Society. The deci**sion** to have the Society also seek incorpora**tion** under state law was included in Dempsey's announce**ment**. Incorpora**tion**, she said, will encourage more enroll**ment** of members because it will result in the elimina**tion** of any individual legal responsibility arising in connec**tion** with the Society's action against ferret abusers.	The Good Ferret Protectors Society is operating again, Executive Director Hazyl Dempsey announced today. The Society also decided to incorporate under state law, she said. More members are now expected to enroll because this move will eliminate any individual legal responsibility connected with the Society's action against ferret abusers.

If you were describing a family softball game to a friend, you might say: *Wendy hit a low line drive. Dallas dove, grabbed it, and fired it to first for the out.* Your "professional" version, full of passive and smothered verbs, would go like this: *The hitting of a low line drive was accomplished by Wendy. Interception of the ball was effected by Dallas, and the achievement of its aerial motivation to first base for the out was executed by the same member of the team.*

Would any normal, red-blooded person ever say, *I am in need of a new hard drive?* Yet that same person finds no problem writing, *We are in need of a new strategic plan,* even though starting with *We need* would be more natural, more concise. Nominalizing can quickly mushroom, the smotherer transforming every simple active verb into bloated, stagey phrasing (see Box 3.3).

BOX 3.3

acquire . . . . seek acquisition
adjust . . . . create an adjustment
alter . . . . make alteration
assist. . . . . render assistance
conclude. . . . . come to a conclusion
decide . . . . arrive at a decision
discuss. . . . . engage in a discussion

estimate . . . . offer an estimation

evaluate . . . . perform an evaluation

indicate . . . . give indication

locate . . . . ascertain the location

substitute . . . . make a substitution

undertake . . . . venture an undertaking

RENO TIP 3.1

RENOVATION TIP

One test of readability is to ask, How would I *say* the same thing if my reader were sitting across from me? A club president will write, *Careful thought and deliberation should take place before we go ahead with any decision that involves the initiation and implementation of a monetary cover charge at club-sponsored socials given such a decision might risk the potential accruing of negative publicity and public reaction.* Asked what this means, the club president replies, *Before we ask everyone for money to attend our parties, we should consider how people might react.* If you can orally translate your message into a clearer, more concise message, your original version needs revision.

PLAY NICE

To get your audience to accept your message—not just readily grasp it—you must present a credible, compelling persona, a voice that leads readers to trust and like you. You must demonstrate you are someone of high character whose thought exemplifies decency and integrity complemented by a gracious and humble tone.

Qualify Sensibly

A trustworthy style begins with an accurate and precise expression of thought. Sometimes your thoughts need to be qualified, lest you appear simplistic or dogmatic. This type of qualification enhances your credibility because it portrays you as reasonable. Writers will say, *I think . . . , I believe . . .* , or *I feel . . .* when it is clear they are offering personal opinion. This is more of a nicety, a rhetorical acknowledgment meant to suggest that the writer is not issuing pronouncements but offering a viewpoint with which others may disagree.

Generally, though, you should limit your use of *I.* Even in personal memos and letters, the overuse of *I* can cast you as self-centered. Although *I* is preferable to speaking in third person (*this writer*) or resorting to the imperial *we* (*we found*), it draws attention to the writer and personalizes your text. Excessive use of *I* can undermine the credibility of reports, proposals, research papers, or other documents that must exemplify objectivity.

Although some writers overqualify their ideas in hopes of achieving greater precision and objectivity, many more do so only to protect themselves. They believe that qualification will somehow insulate them against future criticism and blame. *I never said we should do it; I said it was something we could potentially consider doing or not doing.* Resist the temptation to seek refuge behind a wall of *apparently, appears, approximately, generally, may, maybe, might, perhaps, possibly, seems,* and *usually.* From the very cautious comes the double and triple hedge. *It **appears perhaps** it **may** be **possible** for me to limit my use of qualifying words.* Four qualifying words—*appears, perhaps, may,* and *possible*—in a single sentence? Any one word would suffice. By overqualifying, the writer comes across as timid and not quite trustworthy.

Some writers go the opposite direction. Desperately wanting to sound confident, they overstate their case and become insufferable. Their tone is that of the know-it-all. *My many years of executive experience and my numerous leadership awards received over the past two decades allow me to expertly assess your situation and to tell you where you have made some naive mistakes I am happy to help you correct because I feel an obligation to . . . yada, yada, yada.* And how many times have we seen stunts like these:

- Any intelligent, rational person can see that my position is correct.

  Right, only an idiot would disagree with you. Nice try.
- Any idiot can see that my position is correct.

  Now I'm an idiot because I agree with you. Ok, then, I disagree with you.

If your ideas or arguments are strong, they do not require prefacing that tells the audience just how good they are. You do not need to add: *A great example that supports my case . . . , Another very logical reason why I believe . . . , A point that beautifully illustrates what I've been saying . . .* Let the ideas or arguments speak for themselves; keep the applause signs at bay.

It is also unnecessary to negatively annotate the other side's ideas or arguments, however woefully weak. State and refute the idea or argument without engaging in this sort of battering: *My opponent has come to the silly and ridiculous conclusion that most paintings are overpriced because . . .* A single, carefully chosen word can be far more suggestive. *Curiously, my opponent has concluded that most paintings are overpriced because their price far exceeds the cost of their materials (the canvas and the paint).*

Treat Others Fairly

Intent and function, as noted in Chapter 1, are not the same. The effects of one's words or actions do not necessarily prove a congruent intent. When people misfire, it is seldom because they try to fail. Assigning evil motives to your subjects solely because their words or actions went awry is fallacious and unfair. In the absence of knowing something about your subject's intent, it is best to keep your message focused on what you do know for sure—what happened—which usually provides more than enough grist for critique.

It is also prudent to refrain from the practice of distorting information to build your case. Adapting penny-wise and pound-foolish tactics, many writers mischaracterize the views of others. Their frequent use of the straw man argument serves as a good example. The straw man argument is a fabrication that distorts your opponent's position to make it easier to refute. Like a straw man, the mischaracterization is a flimsy fake you can pick apart.

Your opponent says, for example, that consenting adults should be allowed to view adult pornography in the privacy of their homes. The straw man characterization: *The other side would like to legalize pornography so children can stare at naked adults all day long.* In other words, your opponent is a dangerous extremist who cannot be trusted.

Or your opponent maintains that pornography needs to be more strictly regulated to protect young children. The straw man characterization: *The other side, which obviously does not believe in the First Amendment and never has, wants to control our personal lives and dictate everything we can and cannot watch.* In other words, your opponent is a dangerous extremist who cannot be trusted.

Straw man arguments ultimately impugn the writer's credibility. A better tactical approach, and a more noble one, would be to practice the opposite: describe the other side's position so accurately that anyone holding it would agree with your portrayal. Then refute the position with strong, ethically bound arguments. Treating the views of others with this kind of respect and dignity raises your stature and potential to persuade.

Recognize That Women Exist

Nearly as offensive as the straw man argument, gender-specific pronouns (he or she; him or her; his or hers) alienate many readers, who view such pronouns as stereotypical. In response, more and more companies, organizations, and publications have adopted policies against the use of sexist pronouns, which are seen as insensitive and outdated. Fortunately, you can easily change gender-specific pronouns.

The three best options, when possible, are to replace unnecessary pronouns with other words, to restructure the sentence so that the pronouns are not needed, or to pluralize singular subjects.

REPLACE UNNECESSARY PRONOUNS.

ORIGINAL	Each itinerant editor must submit **his** travel request.
REVISION	Each itinerant editor must submit a travel request.
ORIGINAL	**His** company budget limited the technical writer to 75-word instructional manuals.
REVISION	The company budget limited the technical writer to 75-word instructional manuals.

RESTRUCTURE THE SENTENCE.

ORIGINAL	If a Chief Financial Officer is loved, **she** is never forgotten.
REVISION	A Chief Financial Officer who is loved is never forgotten.

ORIGINAL   Any administrative assistant can be successful if **he** works hard.

REVISION   Any administrative assistant who works hard can be successful.

ORIGINAL   Every IT consultant should be computer literate if **she** expects to be hired.

REVISION   Every IT consultant who expects to be hired should be computer literate.

PLURALIZE SINGULAR SUBJECTS.

ORIGINAL   Each itinerant editor must submit **his** travel request.

REVISED   Itinerant editors must submit their travel requests.

Other options:

USE THE PHRASE *HE OR SHE*.

Sometimes only *he or she*, *he/she*, *his or her*, or *his/her* will do. Awkward and wordy, this option is best used sparingly. S/he is better, but it has never quite caught on.

ALTERNATE GENDER-SPECIFIC PRONOUNS.

Use the male pronoun for one example and the female pronoun for another, or, as found in some children's books, use male pronouns in one chapter and female pronouns in the next. Alternating gender-specific pronouns, however, can be disorienting.

IGNORE THE GRAMMATICAL RULE.

A grammatically incorrect but increasingly popular solution, even with some linguists (but not endorsed here), is to go ahead and use plural pronouns when their referent nouns are singular. *Each itinerant editor must submit their travel request.*

RENO TIP **3.2**

RENOVATION TIP

James Thurber said, "Don't get it right, just get it written." Finish your entire draft, no matter how rough the copy may be, before beginning any major rewriting. Fixating over flawed sentences and paragraphs at this point in the creative process interrupts the flow of ideas. It is also easier to revise once you can see where all your thoughts fall, further sparing you from reworking material you may end up deleting. On your first draft, include just about everything (it is easier later to cut than to add), which will allow you to work through your thoughts and revise them more effectively.

Chapter 3

EXERCISES

EXERCISE 1. Fast start these slow starts by cutting and/or revising the offending material.

A. I will now present my objections to your proposal, which come in the form of five reasons.
B. In addressing your concerns about why I have been late to class eight times, I would like to say that I have never come to class late intentionally.
C. You have asked me to give you my responses to the ten questions you have posed of me, which I will now do.
D. There are no social dating websites devoted to matching Christians, Jews, and Muslims who share a mutual interest in writing clearly, concisely, and compellingly.
E. There are some sentences that may need to start with *there are*, but this is not one of them.

EXERCISE 2. Change the following paragraph, now in passive voice, into active voice.

The A+ on my last paper was deserved. My arguments were developed and structured flawlessly; they were also sequenced beautifully. And my paper was punctuated perfectly. Most of all, my personality—thoughtful, organized, detailed, and modest—was captured by my essay.

EXERCISE 3. Change the following paragraph, now in active voice, into passive voice.

At first, I thought my professor did not like me because she insisted I needed to improve my writing skills. She suggested several ways how I could get better. I followed all her advice. I improved my writing skills, and several employers took me more seriously. Although most of my friends received one or two job offers after graduation, five companies offered me a job. Because of my strong writing skills, my current employer just promoted me again. Now I think my professor did like me.

EXERCISE 4. Change the nominalized verb in each of these sentences back to its original verb form and delete the no longer needed verb.

A. By next week, the school will arrive at a decision about whether to conduct an investigation of its athletic program.
B. You must make payment of your parking fines.
C. The play, now six hours long, needs to come to an end.
D. Sharon has been a consistent winner of our Writer of the Month award.
E. Students who know how to fix nominalized verbs should render assistance to those who don't.

EXERCISE 5. Revise and significantly shorten this memo, sent from The Boss from Hell to 250 employees, by editing sentences and deleting others.

I was completely shocked to learn that many of you have brazenly decided not to attend our annual holiday party, scheduled for the evening of December 24.

I have led many companies with extraordinary success over the years, and I have never in my entire professional life ever experienced such employee disdain for a company-sponsored event. I believe that if someone is so detached and removed from this company that he would rather not participate in our most well-meaning of corporate events, he obviously should reconsider why he is working for us. I think everyone needs to be more considerate and understanding of the goodwill this company is trying to build by holding an annual holiday party and spending a lot of money it didn't have to. We had hoped that everyone would have the chance to socialize and join in the holiday spirit.

I have been told it may be possible we should not perhaps have scheduled the party for the evening of December 24. I have heard rumors that many people wanted to attend but had other commitments. If that is so, I can reschedule the event to December 10. I have no problem doing this because that's the kind of person I am. Everything I do is out of the goodness of my heart and my concern for my employees.

4 Constructing Paragraphs and Pages

The intent and function of all writing, as noted earlier, is persuasive. The writer seeks to capture and hold the reader's attention, while building a case for why the reader should believe and accept the writer's message. Whether intended or not, the message functions persuasively by ultimately altering audience beliefs, attitudes, and behaviors. By the same token, all messages also contain informative elements.

It is thus useful to categorize messages along the lines of an informative–persuasive continuum that allows for distinguishing between those that seek *primarily to inform* through the description and explanation of ideas versus those that seek *primarily to persuade* through arguments designed to posit, strengthen, or change audience beliefs, attitudes, and behaviors.

STATE YOUR PURPOSE LIKE YOU MEAN IT

What is the most important thing you want your audience to know or do? Put another way, if you knew your audience would read only one sentence of your entire message, what sentence would you choose? The answer is your purpose statement. In a single sentence, it conveys the gist of what you are asking of your reader.

Knowing your overall purpose is crucial because it controls everything you say. Worded properly, it helps you organize your material and stay focused. A poorly worded purpose statement runs the risk of confusing, or even losing, your reader before you start.

Good purpose statements meet the following five criteria:

1. *Your Purpose Statement Should Specifically and Precisely Summarize the Goal of Your Message.* If it just introduces your topic, the reader is given little sense of your purpose. You must specifically and precisely forecast what you are about to describe/explain or argue.

ORIGINAL   This memo deals with the matter of our dress code.

REVISION A   This memo describes the proposed changes to our dress code. (informative)

REVISION B   This memo maintains that the proposed changes to our dress code will result in more staring and less work. (persuasive)

Just as some purpose statements reveal no purpose, others are so general and vague that the reader fares only slightly better in knowing what specifically and precisely concerns the writer.

ORIGINAL   Let's take a look at our dress code.

REVISION   Let's review the 19 rules of our dress code.

ORIGINAL   Something needs to be done about our dress code.

REVISION   Our dress code should be revised to prevent employees from wearing 100% polyester.

2. *Your Purpose Statement, Especially in a Persuasive Message, Should Express a Sense of Conviction and Confidence.* Trying to render your purpose more palatable by softening its presentation with wimpy wording will only result in you being seen as weak and uncertain.

ORIGINAL   We should consider revising our dress code.

REVISION   We should revise our dress code.

ORIGINAL   Our dress code may have a problem relative to productivity.

REVISION   Our dress code does not promote productivity.

Your sense of conviction and confidence, however, should not extend to coloring the wording of your proposition with language that assumes the acceptance of arguments you have yet to make.

ORIGINAL   We should revise our silly dress code.

REVISION   We should revise our dress code.

ORIGINAL   Our outdated dress code does not promote productivity.

REVISION   Our dress code does not promote productivity.

Certainly, you can argue the dress code should be revised *because* it is silly, or the dress code does not promote productivity *because* it is outdated. But these arguments must be developed, not presupposed. Your proposition should be neutrally worded so that its language does not give an unfair advantage to proponents of either side.

3. *Your Purpose Statement Should Be Succinct and Not Overly Detailed.* It is fine to combine your purpose statement and your supporting main ideas or main arguments into one sentence if your purpose statement and supporting main ideas or main arguments are short enough. On the other hand, you should not overwhelm your readers with a summary of subideas or subarguments in your purpose statement. Purpose statements crowded with too many elements can be difficult to grasp. Instead, keep your purpose statement short and then follow up, if necessary, with more detailed sentences relating to your purpose.

ORIGINAL   The Piranha Rescue Habitat will hold a manager's workshop to discuss how to recruit new employees from three sectors—private, nonprofit, and government—and will include a discussion of which magazines, television stations, and social networking websites to use for advertizing; how to read chronological, functional, and audio-visual resumes; and what types of closed and open-ended questions to ask in interviews.

REVISION   The Piranha Rescue Habitat will hold a manager's workshop to discuss how to recruit new employees, including where to advertize, how to read resumes, and what to ask in interviews. More specifically, the workshop will discuss which media to use when you advertise . . .
Or
The Piranha Rescue Habitat will hold a manager's workshop to discuss how to recruit new employees. It will include where to advertize, how to read resumes, and what to ask in interviews. More specifically, the workshop will discuss . . .

ORIGINAL   Professor Hehl should be fired because he is disorganized in his lectures, PowerPoint slides, and Blackboard materials; he grades unfairly, whether the test is essay, short answer, multiple choice, or true/false; and he abhors research and researchers, regardless of their discipline or methodological approach.

REVISION   Professor Hehl should be fired because he is disorganized, grades unfairly, and abhors research. More specifically, he is disorganized because . . .

Your purpose statement should not summarize "the how" when you present an informative message that describes an existing policy or when you present a persuasive message that proposes a policy.

ORIGINAL   Rite University teaches writing across the curriculum by training all professors, via on-campus and online workshops and seminars taught by campus experts, on how to evaluate writing and how to include writing assignments in all their courses, whether they be lower division, upper division, or graduate level.

REVISION   Rite University teaches writing across the curriculum.

ORIGINAL   The company should prohibit employees from cross-dressing during normal business hours by first changing the rules of the Employee Handbook and then posting signs throughout the building that read, *Dress like a man, Dress like woman.*

REVISION   The company should prohibit employees from cross-dressing during normal business hours.

4. *Your Purpose Statement Should Be Worded as a Short Declarative Sentence, Not as a Question.* A declarative sentence immediately states your position; a question does not.

ORIGINAL	What caused Tuesday's high rate of absenteeism?
REVISION	Monday Night Football caused Tuesday's high rate of absenteeism.
ORIGINAL	How do employees feel about the new rule against interoffice dating?
REVISION A	Employees approve of the new rule against interoffice dating.
REVISION B	Married employees are the only ones opposed to the new rule against interoffice dating.
ORIGINAL	Does the university have the right to raise tuition every month?
REVISION A	The university has the right to raise tuition every month.
REVISION B	The university does not have the right to raise tuition every month.
ORIGINAL	Should the university charge $95,000 a year in tuition?
REVISION A	The university should charge $95,000 a year in tuition.
REVISION B	The university should not charge $95,000 a year in tuition.

5. *Your Purpose Statement Should Contain One Central Idea or Central Argument, Not Two or Three.* A purpose statement having more than one central idea or central argument means you have more than one purpose. This can confuse your reader, who must reconcile two or more different sets of supporting ideas or arguments brought together in service of two or more different purposes. It is easier for readers to follow along when they are asked to process one concept at a time.

ORIGINAL	I would like to describe the university's new requirement that all students be proficient in three languages, as well as explain the university's tuition refund policy for students who drop out before the second week of classes.
REVISION A	I would like to describe the university's new requirement that all students be proficient in three languages.
REVISION B	I would like to explain the university's tuition refund policy for students who drop out before the second week of classes.
ORIGINAL	The company should extend the lunch break to three hours and provide stock options to all employees.
REVISION A	The company should extend the lunch break to three hours.
REVISION B	The company should provide stock options to all employees.

Choosing between purposes does not mean you have to ignore any. You could, for example, write about extending the lunch break and about providing stock options—just not in the same message. The two purposes are unrelated and best addressed separately.

If you have several closely related purposes, try consuming them under one overarching purpose statement. *Not* like this:

> ORIGINAL   The Journalism Department should offer more courses in writing for social networking websites, setting up websites, and creating blogs; establish paid internship programs with local media outlets; hire younger, cooler faculty who are not so stuck in the dark ages of hardcopy newspapers; and recognize that it is okay for students to want to become famous and make a lot of money practicing journalism.

This purpose statement is not helpful because it throws out several arguments without any unifying thread that would help the reader see how they articulate and are subordinate to a larger purpose. A better statement of purpose might read:

> REVISION   The Journalism Department should significantly change how it teaches classes and mentors students. [You can then follow up.] More specifically, the Journalism Department needs to offer additional courses in writing for social networking websites, setting up websites, . . .

Note that *teaches classes* and *mentors students* are so closely related they are treated as one, not two, ideas, in the same way that *spaghetti and meatballs is* [not *are*] *my favorite meal*. It is also common to treat these ideas as singular: *Taking courses in the Journalism Department represents* **cruel and unusual** *punishment. Hiring faculty who know nothing about social networking is a waste of* **time and money**.

You may not know your exact purpose until you have sorted out your entire message. Viewing all your main ideas or main arguments at once enables you to grasp the central idea or argument—your purpose statement—that unites them. In the example given, the listing of everything wrong with the Journalism Department facilitates the process of synthesis, making it easier to conclude that the department *should significantly change how it teaches classes and mentors students*.

When you are not sure of your purpose statement, starting with a tentative statement can help you sort out and develop material; the statement can then be revised as you work through the body of your message. It is also a good idea to reconsider your purpose statement *after* you have finished drafting your message. Ask yourself, Does my purpose statement encompass all my main ideas or main arguments? If not, can it be revised accordingly, or must I change my message to be consistent with my purpose statement? Does my purpose statement speak to one or more main ideas or main arguments not covered in my message? If so, how can I bring my purpose statement in line with my message or vice versa?

BUILD THEM (PARAGRAPHS) RIGHT AND THEY (READERS) WILL COME

Bottomline Your Main Ideas or Main Arguments

Your purpose statement should appear in your paper's introduction, usually in the first paragraph. Your purpose statement may be the lead sentence of the paragraph, or it may come later in the paragraph if brief background information is first needed. If you have a lot of background material helpful but not crucial to understanding your message, place it after your opening paragraph so you do not lose your reader with a barrage of detail at the onset.

Stating your purpose in the first paragraph increases the chances it will be seen. Although readers often skip and skim message content, they usually read all or most of the first paragraph. Knowing your purpose from the start gives readers an immediate point of reference for everything that follows. It allows for easy reading of your message because it is clear where you are going and how everything relates. Conversely, when you build up to your purpose, your message is harder to follow because the reader must connect the dots along the way. Readers who tire of the extra work may not stick around.

Regrettably, much writing is composed as if it were a short story or a novel. The author creates suspense, holding back the purpose statement until the end. If you are writing a mystery, this is the right approach. You introduce clues (evidence) throughout the story and then reveal the murderer (the conclusion) in the closing pages. Mystery readers enjoy the challenge of figuring out who did it because that is how they are entertained. But in our everyday routines, we have too much to read in too little time. We are not amused by detective work. Quickly we want to know, *Who is the murderer?* If we are interested in the details, we will read on, but with the benefit of knowing beforehand what the subsequent clues support.

Why is so much writing organized backward in the sense that writers fail to first state their purpose? Perhaps it is because most research and investigation follow a *climactic* pattern: You collect pieces of information (data) and then look to see what overall conclusion they support. The mistake is following the same sequence—starting with data and then building toward a climax or conclusion—when you write.

Ordinarily, most nonfiction messages should be organized *anti-climactically*: Your overall conclusion (worded as your purpose statement) comes first, followed by your supporting data. Essentially, you invert the steps of your research or investigative process and begin by announcing your conclusion before explaining how you arrived at it. Organizing your writing this way makes it easier for the reader to follow your message.

RENO TIP	**4.1**

RENOVATION TIP

A climactic writing pattern may be appropriate for announcing "bad" news, such as laying off an employee, canceling the Christmas party, or disclosing you just dropped out of school. In these cases, starting with your purpose statement—*Pack up your bags, you're no longer part of the team; Sorry, but we're not celebrating Christmas this year; Dear Mom and Dad, I left school yesterday and will be joining a carnival tomorrow*—can cast you as cold and insensitive, making an already trying situation worse. A climactic approach tries to prepare the audience for the bad news by gradually leading up to it.

Near or at the end of your paper's introduction, it is a good idea to give a *preview*, which is a summary of the main ideas or main arguments you will present. The body of your message, which follows your introduction, reintroduces and develops these main ideas or main arguments.

Frequently, writers will lead up to the paragraph's main idea or main argument or, worse, embed it in the middle of the paragraph. The main idea or main argument should be extracted and repositioned as the first sentence of the paragraph.

Think of your main idea or main argument as the essence, the *bottom line*, of the paragraph. You can determine the bottom line by asking, What overall generalization or conclusion do the sentences in the paragraph support? The answer is your bottom line, expressed by the *topic sentence*. The topic sentence usually appears as the first sentence of the paragraph. (Chapter 5, which revisits topic sentences from another perspective, discusses when you would not position your topic sentence at the top of the paragraph, as well as when you would not need an explicit topic sentence.)

In an informative message, your introductory paragraph usually summarizes what you will be describing or explaining before you actually provide any description or explanation. As indicated earlier, your purpose statement may be the first sentence of this paragraph, or it may come later if preceded by brief background information. You may also want to use the beginning of your first paragraph to grab the readers' attention and establish the significance of your topic. In much longer reports and academic papers, your purpose statement may appear in the last paragraph of a multiparagraph introduction if essential context for the statement must first be developed. Regardless of the length of your introduction, however, it houses your purpose statement.

If you were informing readers of your company's new process for travel reimbursement, you could start with something like this:

FIRST PARAGRAPH.   This memo describes the three steps involved in our new Travel Reimbursement Procedure when staying at beachfront destinations [purpose statement]. These steps include (1) getting your supervisor's approval before taking the trip, (2) completing our new travel reimbursement form upon your return, and (3) attaching all travel receipts to the form [preview].

In addition, this paragraph could include background material on what motivated the change in policy and when did it take effect.

Each subsequent paragraph of your message would advance your purpose statement by developing one of its supporting main ideas. Paragraphs two, three, and four would begin by bottomlining steps 1, 2, and 3, respectively, with the rest of the paragraph elaborating upon each step. Your topic sentences might read:

SECOND PARAGRAPH, FIRST SENTENCE. The first and most important step in the new Travel Reimbursement Procedure is making sure you have your supervisor's approval before taking your trip.

THIRD PARAGRAPH, FIRST SENTENCE. You will also need to complete the new travel reimbursement form upon your return.

FOURTH PARAGRAPH, FIRST SENTENCE. The final step in the new procedure requires you to attach all travel receipts to the form.

Let's turn to persuasive messages and a different example. In your first paragraph, you propose, say, that *Roger should be fired as chief executive officer (CEO) because he is dishonest, cannot manage, and is emotionally unstable.* Here, your purpose statement and supporting arguments can be combined into one sentence because they are short enough to be easily processed as a single thought. The paragraphs that follow would bottomline your main arguments with topic sentences, such as these:

SECOND PARAGRAPH, FIRST SENTENCE. Foremost, Roger should be fired because he is dishonest.

THIRD PARAGRAPH, FIRST SENTENCE. Another reason why Roger should be fired is that he cannot manage.

FOURTH PARAGRAPH, FIRST SENTENCE. If being dishonest and a poor manager were not enough, Roger is also emotionally unstable. (No doubt he does not write well either.)

Effective bottomlining can sometimes be a matter of just repositioning your purpose statement, re-paragraphing your text, and adding a few helpful words. In the following example, neither the writer's purpose nor the supporting arguments are bottomlined. Instead, they are all combined into one paragraph, making it difficult to differentiate them.

ORIGINAL I'd like to discuss the matter of staff support in our office. For many months now, the Center for Effective and Efficient Management has been short-staffed, which has led to its deteriorating performance. The center has become inefficient. Clients should not have to wait a week or longer, as they do now, before hearing from us. We need to answer client questions about our consulting services promptly. The center has become unprofessional. Our work product is often messy and incomplete. I know that the staff is stretched too far and does not have the time to carefully prepare and edit e-mails and letters to clients. However, it reflects poorly on our image. In the end, it is not good for business. The cost of hiring more staff will be offset by the financial benefits of reestablishing our clients' trust and confidence. Many of our clients are now starting to go elsewhere for our services, as shown by last quarter's decline in sales. I propose we hire at least three new employees.

In the revision of this example, the first sentence, which says little, is deleted. It masquerades as a purpose statement, albeit a poor one that has no point of view. It is upstaged by the real purpose statement coming at the end of the message. The three main arguments are separated into paragraphs and bottomlined so they can be distinguished from one another. Adding some text and labeling the main arguments drive home the message.

REVISION   ~~I'd like to discuss the matter of staff support in our office.~~ For many months now, the Center for Effective and Efficient Management has been short-staffed, which has led to its deteriorating performance. **To remedy the problem,** I propose we hire at least three new employees. **More specifically, here's why:**

First, the center has become inefficient. Clients should not have to wait a week or longer, as they do now, before hearing from us. We need to answer client questions about our consulting services promptly.

Second, the center has become unprofessional. Our work product is often messy and incomplete. I know that the staff is stretched too far and does not have the time to carefully prepare and edit e-mails and letters to clients. However, it reflects poorly on our image. In the end, it is not good for business.

Finally, the cost of hiring more staff will be offset by the financial benefits of reestablishing our clients' trust and confidence. Many of our clients are now starting to go elsewhere for our services, as shown by last quarter's decline in sales.

Organize Evidence into Piles and Subpiles

ROGER SHOULD BE FIRED AS CEO.   When necessary, main ideas or main arguments should be broken into subideas or subarguments to make it easier to process your message. In proposing that *Roger should be fired as CEO,* you might have several pieces of evidence (facts, examples, statistics, and testimony) relating to Roger's dishonesty. You could offer this evidence by simply saying, *Sixteen pieces of evidence support my conclusion.* But this would be a less-than-compelling presentation. Your evidence needs to be organized.

You can arrive at your subideas and subarguments more easily by first structuring your evidence into piles and subpiles. One way to begin is by grouping similar-themed pieces of evidence. Let's take the 16 pieces of evidence and represent them with Os:

<pre>
O   O   O   O
O   O   O   O
O   O   O   O
O   O   O   O
</pre>

Now, let's organize this large pile into subpiles based on the commonalities the evidence shares. If certain pieces speak to Roger being a liar, let's put them into a subpile (Ol) and then name the subpile based on what it supports: *Roger lies.* The evidence that Roger cheats (Oc) and steals (Os) can also be grouped into subpiles and named. To review, first identify all the pieces of evidence in the large pile:

<pre>
Os   Oc   Ol   Os
Ol   Oc   Os   Ol
Oc   Ol   Oc   Os
Ol   Os   Ol   Oc
</pre>

Then put the evidence into themed subpiles and name the subpiles:

Subpile 1:   Ol, Ol, Ol, Ol, Ol, Ol   =   Roger lies. (subargument A)

Subpile 2:   Oc, Oc, Oc, Oc, Oc   =   Roger cheats. (subargument B)

Subpile 3:   Os, Os, Os, Os, Os   =   Roger steals. (subargument C)

Naming your subpiles generates the wording that will express your subideas or subarguments. This wording should adhere to the same criteria for formulating a purpose statement: It must specifically and precisely summarize your position with conviction and confidence; succinctly address one idea or argument; and, generally, state your position as a declarative sentence, which helps capture the essence of your thought by framing it as an action (for an example of when you might elect not to start your paragraph with a declarative sentence, see Chapter 5, Exercise 3).

Subideas or subarguments essentially break down your main ideas or main arguments into related parts around which it is easier to organize your evidence and build your paragraphs.

SECOND PARAGRAPH.   Foremost, Roger should be fired because he is dishonest. This dishonesty takes several forms. Roger lies [followed by evidence: Ol, Ol, Ol, Ol, Ol, Ol]. Roger also cheats [followed by evidence: Oc, Oc, Oc, Oc, Oc]. Yet another way Roger is dishonest is that he steals [followed by evidence: Os, Os, Os, Os, Os].

In a short message, you may need only a paragraph to develop each of your main ideas or main arguments. But when you have a potentially unwieldy paragraph that includes extensive subideas or subarguments, such as the one just discussed, it is better to break the paragraph into more than one.

SECOND PARAGRAPH, IN ENTIRETY.   Foremost, Roger should be fired because he is dishonest. This dishonesty takes several forms.

THIRD PARAGRAPH, FIRST SENTENCE.   Roger lies. (followed by evidence)

FOURTH PARAGRAPH, FIRST SENTENCE.   Roger also cheats. (followed by evidence)

FIFTH PARAGRAPH, FIRST SENTENCE.   Yet another way that Roger is dishonest is that he steals. (followed by evidence)

The process by which you arrive at your subideas or subarguments actually comes into play earlier when determining your main ideas or main arguments. Looking at all your evidence, you would have concluded that it falls into three themed piles: Roger is dishonest, Roger cannot manage, and Roger is emotionally unstable. Put another way, the evidence forms bodies of support for different conclusions, which become your main ideas or main arguments.

THE EARTHQUAKE ADVERSELY AFFECTED OUR FAMILY. How your evidence shapes the formation and wording of your main ideas/main arguments or subideas/subarguments can be seen in this example of how an earthquake affected a family:

1. The garage roof collapsed.
2. I fractured my right index finger.
3. Our desktop computer broke into 86 pieces.
4. Our killer shark aquarium now leaks in three places.
5. Several of our clothes fell off their hangers.
6. Our favorite Elvis statue lost its head.
7. The frame broke on the largest of our Lady Gaga velvet paintings.
8. Our cat sprained her left foot.
9. The upstairs wall-to-wall shag carpet was stained in several places.
10. Our dog chipped a tooth.
11. The wedding pictures from my sixth (and second best) marriage burst into flames.
12. My notes from my first college composition class were thrown everywhere.
13. My wife suffered a separated shoulder.
14. The main gas line snapped.
15. Our dining room table cracked.
16. The wooden patio doors were scratched.

Organizing this evidence begins with the grouping of pieces that share obvious commonalities. From there, you work your way down, refining your organizational piles into subpiles, sub-subpiles, and beyond, if necessary.

Start by asking, Of the listed items, which are similar in nature? The glaring answer is that some are living objects (people and pets), while others are inanimate objects (of various sorts). Let's begin with the living:

2. I fractured my right index finger.
8. Our cat sprained her left foot.
10. Our dog chipped a tooth.
13. My wife suffered a separated shoulder.

These four pieces of evidence go into a pile, which you name *The earthquake caused injuries to our family.* But wait, can we break this pile into two subpiles? After all, the earthquake injured two different life forms: humans and pets. Wouldn't it be better to discuss human injuries before pet injuries? The paragraph following your introduction might then look like this:

SECOND PARAGRAPH. The earthquake caused injuries to our family. My wife suffered a separated shoulder, which was very painful and took three months to heal. I fractured my right index finger and was unable to pitch in my Over-75 Super Senior Softball League. Meanwhile, our pets endured injuries as well. Paula, our cat, sprained her left foot and has been unable to catch mice for weeks. Our beautiful show dog, Simon, chipped a tooth and will need dental work before he can compete again in dog shows.

Although the remaining pile of evidence is quite large, these four items clearly reference house damage:

1. The garage roof collapsed.
9. The upstairs wall-to-wall shag carpet was stained in several places.
14. The main gas line snapped.
16. The wooden patio doors were scratched.

The second main pile of evidence can now be named *The earthquake damaged our house.* To lump the four supporting pieces of evidence without distinction, however, would imply they are all of equal significance. Breaking the pile into subpiles—major and minor damage—allows the writer to emphasize the *major* damage.

THIRD PARAGRAPH. The earthquake also damaged our house. Major damage included the collapsed garage roof and the snapped main gas line. Estimates to repair the garage roof range from $3,000 to $4,500. We may incur more costs because the garage will be unprotected from the weather until we repair the roof. Fortunately, the main gas line will not be as expensive to fix as the roof, but it does pose a major danger. Overworked city repair crews have not had time to replace the line. As if all this were not enough, minor damage to the house will add to our cost, inconvenience, and time. We will need to repair the wooden patio doors scratched by a falling tree branch, and we will have to hire a professional to clean the wall-to-wall shag carpet, which was stained in several places.

Much like a puzzle that gets easier to complete as you go along, a message becomes easier to structure when you have fewer pieces of evidence left to organize. It is now apparent the remaining evidence describes personal property and includes items that incurred irreparable damage, *major damage*, or **no damage** (they were scattered):

3. Our desktop computer broke into 86 pieces

4. *Our killer shark aquarium now leaks in three places.*

5. Several of our clothes fell off their hangers.

6. Our favorite Elvis statue lost its head.

7. *The frame broke on the largest of our Lady Gaga velvet paintings.*

11. The wedding pictures from my sixth (and second best) marriage burst into flames.

12. My notes from my first college composition class were thrown everywhere.

15. *Our dining room table cracked.*

The process of organizing evidence into piles exposes which ideas or arguments are not worth pursuing. Evidence of falling clothes and disarrayed notes supports an argument that is trivial in the larger context of the earthquake's effects. To talk about scattered items in the same breath as damaged items wastes time and lowers the writer's credibility. It is better to omit them.

FOURTH PARAGRAPH.   In addition to injuring our family and damaging our house, the earthquake took a heavy toll on our personal property. Some items incurred irreparable damage, such as our desktop computer, which broke into 86 pieces; our favorite Elvis statue, which lost its head; and the wedding pictures from my sixth (and second best) marriage, which burst into flames. Other items incurred major damage and will require repairs, such as our killer shark aquarium, the frame on the largest of our Lady Gaga velvet paintings, and our dining room table.

RENO TIP **4.2**

RENOVATION TIP

A good test of whether you have effectively bottomlined your main ideas or main arguments is to have someone read your first paragraph and then just the first sentence of each paragraph that follows. A well-organized message will make considerable (not complete) sense even after such an abbreviated reading.

EMBRACE YOUR OUTLINE

Grouping ideas or arguments into piles, subpiles, and even sub-subpiles enables you to produce an effective outline, which facilitates the shaping of your message and the enhancing of its readability. But just having an outline does not necessarily lead to a well-organized message. It is the quality of the outline that counts: whether it illuminates the interplay of your thoughts and uncovers what should be highlighted, downplayed, or eliminated.

Putting together a quality outline is harder than it looks. An outline is not a bulleted list or a list simply prefaced by Roman and Arabic numbers and upper- and lowercase letters. An outline organizes your ideas or arguments from general to specific by ranking their level of importance in terms of which are superior and which are subordinate. It permits you to see how your ideas or arguments structurally relate and how their presentation should be developed and sequenced.

Example 4.1 shows how you would outline the body of "The earthquake adversely affected our family."

4.1 Student Example

I. The earthquake injured our family members. [main argument]
   A. People were injured. [subargument]
      1. My wife suffered a separated shoulder. [evidence]
      2. I fractured my right index finger. [evidence]
   B. Pets were injured. [subargument]
      1. Our cat sprained her left foot. [evidence]
      2. Our dog chipped a tooth. [evidence]
II. The earthquake damaged our house.
   A. Our house incurred major damage.
      1. The garage roof collapsed.
      2. The main gas line snapped.
   B. Our house incurred minor damage.
      1. The wooden patio doors were scratched.
      2. The upstairs wall-to-wall shag carpet was stained in several places.
III. The earthquake damaged our personal property.
   A. Items incurred irreparable damage.
      1. Our desktop house computer broke into 86 pieces.
      2. Our favorite Elvis statue lost its head.
      3. The wedding pictures from my sixth (and second best) marriage burst into flames.
   B. Items incurred major damage.
      1. Our killer shark aquarium now leaks in three places.
      2. The frame broke on the largest of our Lady Gaga velvet paintings.
      3. Our dining room table cracked.

Although each of the main arguments (I, II, and III) in Example 4.1 contains two subarguments (A and B), a main idea or main argument may need to be divided into more than two subideas or subarguments, or it may not need to be divided at all. A main idea or main argument, however, cannot have a single subidea or subargument any more than you can "divide" a stick into one. For example, if you were to eliminate subargument II.B, you could *not* structure your second main argument this way:

> **II.** The earthquake damaged our house.
>> **A.** Our house incurred major damage.
>>> **1.** The garage roof collapsed.
>>> **2.** The main gas line snapped.

Our house incurred major damage is not a subargument; it is a more precise wording of the main argument. The single subargument adds unnecessary structure and diffuses the reader's attention. Deleting it and rewording the main argument corrects the problem.

> **II.** The earthquake caused major damage to our house.
>> **A.** The garage roof collapsed.
>> **B.** The main gas line snapped.

This revised main argument has no subarguments (a pile without subpiles). The two pieces of evidence (A and B) directly support the main argument.

A main idea or main argument should not be broken into smaller piles unless it produces a minimum of two subideas or subarguments that differ— *and* relate in the sense they both support the larger idea or argument to which they are subordinate. A roof collapse may not be the same as a snapped main gas line, but both are evidence of how the earthquake caused major damage to the house.

One way to outline the introduction, body, and conclusion of "Roger should be fired as CEO" is illustrated in Example 4.2.

4.2 Student Example

Introduction

I. Company history shows the type of CEO we need.
  A. Company struggled for years.
  B. Not until Linda, our ninth CEO, took over did company revenues and profits start to climb.
    1. She had integrity.
    2. She knew how to lead.
    3. She was well-adjusted.
II. Our CEO should have the same qualities as Linda. Roger does not.

III. Purpose statement: Roger should be fired as CEO.

IV. Preview: He is dishonest, cannot manage, and is emotionally unstable.

Body

  I. Roger is dishonest.   [main argument]

    A. He lies.   [subargument]

    B. He cheats.   [subargument]

    C. He steals.   [subargument]

  II. Roger cannot manage.

    A. He cannot supervise.

    B. He cannot organize.

    C. He cannot prioritize.

  III. Roger is emotionally unstable.

    A. He is irrational.

    B. He is paranoid.

Conclusion

  I. Summary of arguments:

    A. He is dishonest.

    B. He cannot manage.

    C. He is emotionally unstable.

  II. Repeat purpose statement: Roger should be fired as CEO.

  III. Closing quotations from last two CEOs:

    A. Jim: "No one in America has poorer leadership qualities than Roger." [evidence]

    B. Linda: "For the company to survive, we need quality leadership." [evidence]

The three main arguments why Roger should be fired as CEO must differ in kind, and they do: Dishonesty, poor managerial skills, and emotional instability represent distinct problems independent of one another. The arguments should also share the same overall function, and they do: Each directly supports the purpose statement that Roger should be fired as CEO.

Similarly, your subarguments must be different from, and related to, one another. Take this example:

    I. Roger is dishonest.

      A. He lies.

      B. He cheats.

      C. He steals.

Lying, cheating, and stealing are not the same thing: You can engage in one without engaging in all three. All three acts, however, are forms of dishonesty and thereby represent three unique but complementary parts of a whole.

Should you have only a single subargument why Roger is dishonest, delete the subargument and reword your main argument.

INCORRECT	CORRECT
I. Roger is dishonest.	**I.** Roger lies.
A. He lies.	**A.** evidence
1. evidence	**B.** evidence
2. evidence	**C.** evidence
3. evidence	**D.** evidence
4. evidence	

Finally, the wording of each main argument must be broad enough to encompass its subordinate parts, yet specific enough to reflect its larger thrust. For example:

> **II.** Roger cannot manage.
>
>   **A.** He cannot supervise.
>
>   **B.** He cannot organize.
>
>   **C.** He cannot prioritize.

As a main argument, *Roger cannot manage* is well worded because *to manage* is to supervise, organize, and prioritize; this main argument covers its three subarguments. *Roger cannot boss well,* on the other hand, would be too narrowly worded because it basically repeats one of the subarguments, *He cannot supervise,* while failing to address the other two subarguments. *Roger is incompetent* would be too general because it does not precisely summarize what it means when someone cannot supervise, organize, and prioritize.

Having a stack of main ideas or main arguments is usually a sign you do not have enough subidea or subargument development. What may appear to be several main ideas or main arguments are more likely subideas or subarguments that could be consumed under a single main idea or main argument. Take the previous example and suppose that instead of three main arguments—*Roger is dishonest, Roger cannot manage,* and *Roger is emotionally unstable*—you presented eight:

> **I.** Roger lies.
>
> **II.** Roger cheats.
>
> **III.** Roger steals.
>
> **IV.** Roger cannot supervise.
>
> **V.** Roger cannot organize.
>
> **VI.** Roger cannot prioritize.
>
> **VII.** Roger is irrational.
>
> **VIII.** Roger is paranoid.

This would have been a more difficult message to process because it is not reader friendly. The eight arguments do not benefit from any kind of structural connection that indicates how they relate. In contrast, three main arguments articulated with one another and advanced with subdevelopment, as shown, are easier to process. Organizing your message around fewer main ideas or main arguments speaks to the greater significance of your evidence and what it supports.

Poor organization explains why so many messages are ineffective. For most of us, organization, more than any other aspect in our writing, is the most challenging to master. No matter how great our sentences, they do not always come together as a paragraph, nor do great paragraphs always lead to great pages.

Constructing a well-organized message is difficult because we subvocalize so much of our text. Try as we may to critique our own writing, the structural flaws can easily elude us. Adding to the problem, many writers do not like starting with an outline because they feel it inhibits their creativity. They want to begin writing without boundaries. Yet it is nearly impossible to produce a well-organized, longer message without having a prewriting tool, such as an outline, to guide us at some point in the process.

One solution is a reverse outline: You outline your entire text *after* you complete your first draft. The reverse outline reveals not what you *wanted* to say, but what you *did* say and where you said it. When you compare your purpose statement to your supporting main ideas or main arguments, two problems often emerge: (1) The paragraph's main idea or main argument is also developed under another paragraph's main idea or main argument, or it is sporadically developed throughout the text. (2) One or more of the paragraph's subideas or subarguments has migrated to other paragraphs as support for their main ideas or main arguments. When subideas or subarguments roam about your message, readers are sent in too many confusing, disorienting directions.

Note the misplaced arguments and subarguments in the outline in Example 4.3.

4.3   Student Example

Body

I. Roger is dishonest.

   A. He cheats.

   B. He steals.

   C. He is emotionally unstable.   [repeat of main argument III]

II. Roger cannot manage.

   A. He cannot organize.

   B. He cannot prioritize.

   C. He lies.   [subargument belonging under main argument I]

   D. He is irrational.   [subargument belong under main argument III]

III. Roger is emotionally unstable.

   A. He cannot supervise.   [subargument belonging under main argument II]

   B. He is paranoid.

   C. He is dishonest.   [repeat of main argument I]

Besides pinpointing major organizational problems, a reverse outline can help when you get stuck in the middle of a writing project, unable to move forward. Going back and outlining the ideas or arguments you have covered so far helps you to see where you have been and where you need to go.

"Give me six hours to chop down a tree," Abraham Lincoln said, "and I will spend the first four sharpening the axe." The time you devote to outlining and reverse outlining—sharpening your prewriting tools—will more than pay for itself. A quality outline enables you to write more effectively and efficiently.

Grouping items into piles and subpiles to make them easier to find is something most of us are more experienced at than we realize. One needn't go further than the typical house garage, where it is common to store and organize such items as sports equipment, power tools, gardening equipment and supplies, holiday decorations, and old clothes. These categories (piles) can be separated into subcategories (subpiles), sub-subcategories (sub-subpiles), and more. The sports equipment pile, for instance, could be broken into four subpiles, featuring baseball as one of the subpiles (see Box 4.1).

BOX 4.1   Sports Equipment (pile)

Baseball	Soccer	Tennis	Golf (subpiles)

Gloves (sub-subpile)
    Fielder (sub-sub-subpile)
      Right hand (sub-sub-sub-subpile)
      Left hand (sub-sub-sub-subpile)
    First base
      Right hand
      Left hand
    Catcher
      Right hand
      Left hand

Bats
    Wood
      34 inches
      33 inches
      32 inches
      31 inches
      30 inches
    Aluminum
      34 inches
      33 inches
      32 inches
      31 inches
      30 inches

Baseball	Soccer	Tennis	Golf (subpiles)

Balls
    Baseballs
        New
        Used
    Softballs
        New
            11 inches (sub-sub-sub-sub-subpile)
            12 inches
            16 inches
        Used
            11 inches (sub-sub-sub-sub-subpile)
            12 inches
            16 inches

Batting gloves
    Right hand
    Left hand

Batting helmets
    With earflaps
    Without earflaps

Organizing three-dimensional objects is obviously not quite the same as organizing a paper. You can more readily see the similarities and differences between familiar objects than between sentences. That is true even when the sentences reference objects, let alone when they symbolize more abstract thought, such as beliefs and attitudes. Discerning how your sentences specifically relate and differ from one another requires a keen awareness of what you are trying to say.

Although it is easier organizing objects, as opposed to thoughts, into piles, both activities share the same goal and analytical process. We organize a garage so we can access whatever we need with the least amount of effort and frustration. Similarly, we organize messages to facilitate reading. But unlike when you enter your garage, your readers enter your message with no prior knowledge of what exactly to look for and where to find it. This is all the more reason your structure must guide them. They need to be able to identify your purpose, its sustaining ideas or arguments, and the supporting evidence.

DRIVE HOME YOUR MESSAGE: FORMAT YOUR DOCUMENT

Effective formatting visually reinforces your message. Moreover, it facilitates the reading and comprehension of your message by making it more inviting and accessible. Presented with an unparagraphed block of single-spaced type devoid of any variation in layout or a text formatted into several paragraphs with headings and subheadings, which would you choose? Some forms of writing, such as academic and journalistic, are more conservative about the use of bullets, italics, and boldface. You must know your audience beforehand and adapt accordingly.

Many academic style guides, such as the *Publication Manual of the American Psychological Association* (APA) and *The Chicago Manual of Style* (CMS), give specific directions for formatting headings and subheadings. (The *MLA Handbook for Writers of Research Papers* [MLA] is less prescriptive.) In addition, many companies, institutions, and government entities have their own formatting requirements. Templates that ensure consistency and professionalism are incorporated into the organization's word-processing programs. What is often missing from many of these guidelines, however, is any rationale for why they make sense from a visual communication perspective.

When you are not obligated to follow prescribed formatting guidelines, you can pick from an array of memo, letter, e-mail, and report formats that best meets your needs and tastes. Your format should be consistent, attractive, and inviting to read. You never want to do this:

To: All employees of LuC Press

FROM: Josie Mahoney
Date: August 17, 2011

SUBJECT: RK Gunning Clear Writing Workshop

FROM and SUBJECT are in all upper case letters (all capitals), but To and Date are not; entries are double spaced, except between **FROM** and Date; and only **FROM** is boldfaced. Such inconsistencies mirror a sloppy writer who has no attention to detail. Now consider this version:

TO: All employees of LuC Press
FROM: Josie Mahoney
DATE: August 17, 2011
SUBJECT: RK Gunning Clear Writing Workshop

Consistent fonts, equal spacing, and vertically aligned entries make this version easier to read.

Rely on Headings and Subheadings

To avoid confusion about what your headings and subheadings summarize, position them closer to what they head than to what they follow. If you were formatting a briefer version of *Roger should be fired as CEO*, a double-spaced text with indented paragraphs might look something like the sample provided in Example 4.4.

4.4 Student Example

Lacks Honesty

Foremost, Roger should be fired because he is dishonest. This dishonesty takes

several forms:

He Lies

¶_____

_____

He Cheats

¶_____

_____

He Steals

¶_____

_____

Lacks Management Skills

¶_____

_____

Lacks Emotional Stability

¶_____

_____

Single-spaced text, which is harder to read than double-spaced text, is better suited for shorter messages. In a single-spaced document, you can choose either *block* style, where the entire text is left justified, or *semi-block* style, where each paragraph is indented; both styles double space between paragraphs. Again, headings and subordinate headings must be visually attached to their respective texts. Example 4.5 illustrates the block style.

4.5 Student Example

Lacks Honesty

Foremost, Roger should be fired because he is dishonest. This dishonesty takes several forms:

He Lies

¶_____

_____

¶_____

_____

He Cheats

¶_____

_____

¶_____

_____

He Steals

¶_____

_____

¶_____

_____

Lacks Management Skills

¶_____

_____

Lacks Emotional Stability

¶_____

_____

The formatting in Examples 4.4 and 4.5 improves the readability and appeal of the message in several ways:

1. The headings and subheadings clearly and concisely summarize the writer's viewpoint. They are not simply topics, such as *honesty, management skills*, and *emotional stability*, which would have given readers little direction or heads-up about the arguments to follow. In a persuasive message, your headings and subheadings should be abstracted versions of your main arguments and subarguments; they should not be worded neutrally.

2. The headings are linguistically parallel to one another, as are the subheadings. Wording your headings and subheadings in parallel language shows how they relate to one another, which, in turn, makes them easier for readers to remember. *He lies, He cheats, He steals* share a parallel structure: Each begins with the subject *He* followed by an active verb and no object or complement. The subheadings would not be parallel if *He lies* had been followed by *He has a problem with cheating* and *Stealing is like a hobby to him.*

3. Each of the headings, as well as each of the subheadings, is consistent with one another in terms of font (typeface, point size, and typeface style): Headings and subheadings are in bold upper and lower case letters. All capitals can be tough to read, particularly in full sentences, and should be used only in the shortest of copy, such as headings. In place of all uppercase lettering, consider using a larger point size—for example, Lacks Honesty (14 point) rather than LACKS HONESTY (12 point).

4. The subheadings (*He lies, He cheats, He steals*) are visually subordinate to their main headings. Headings are visually subordinate when they are presented in lower versus upper case, set in smaller versus larger point size, styled regularly versus boldly, left justified versus page centered (usually), or placed in-text versus above-text. Formatting that visually distinguishes headings from subordinate headings helps to reiterate the structure of the idea or argument.

When headings include sub-subheadings (third-level headings), they should be visually subordinate to the second-level headings that precede them. For example, if you were to argue that Roger is guilty of two types of lying—he fabricates facts and he omits facts—you could introduce both sub-subarguments with *in-text* headings. Positioning a heading *in* the text rather than *above* the text reduces the heading's visual prominence because it no longer stands alone. Instead, it becomes part of the text, as shown in Example 4.6.

4.6 Student Example

Lacks Honesty

Foremost, Roger should be fired because he is dishonest. This dishonesty takes several forms.

He Lies

Fabricates facts. _____

_____

Omits facts. _____

_____

---

5. The three headings and three subheadings are visually closer to the texts they head than the texts they follow. Connecting headings and subheadings with their texts aids readability. On the other hand, headings and subheadings that bleed into their texts impair readability. Bolding headings and subheadings, in addition to providing emphasis, helps to separate them from closing trailing texts. When headings and subheadings "float"—when they are equally distanced between the text they follow and the text they head—they can be misread as belonging to the text they follow. Example 4.7 demonstrates how difficult it can be to make quick sense of which headings go with which texts when the spacing gives no clues.

4.7   Student Example

Alabama Victorious at Home

The game went into three overtimes before a trick play decided it.

46–45

Oklahoma Wins by One Point

The controversial ending came in the closing seconds on a snowy field.

Ohio State Loses Narrowly on Last Play

A missed extra point led to a 7-6 score.

Florida Wins Close One

28–27

LSU Takes Game in a Nail Biter

Befriend Bullets and Numbers

Bullets draw attention to selected elements of your message. Once the computer replaced the typewriter, bullets became an available option in various forms, such as dots, open circles, boxes and shadowed boxes, and check marks. Bullets are commonplace in informal writing. Together with other formatting tools, however, they remain less acceptable in formal venues, such as academic writing.

When used correctly, bullets highlight distinct and *equal* parts of a whole. For example,

Good, not necessarily tenured, professors usually possess three [equally important] qualities:
• They are knowledgeable.
• They are conscientious.
• They are accessible.

Our spy pens come in four colors:
• black
• grey
• grey and black
• black and white

If you have subpoints under a bullet, your second-level bullets must be visually subordinate.

Our spy pens come in four colors:
• black
    • black with white gun silhouettes
    • black with green gun silhouettes
    • black with yellow gun silhouettes

- grey
- grey and black
- black and white

The rise of the bullet has also brought overuse and incorrect use. Only the romance challenged, for example, would ever use bullets to segment a narrative.

- Romeo met Juliet.
- They fell in love.
- Their unenlightened parents didn't approve.
- Romeo and Juliet killed themselves.

Two cautionary points about bullets bear emphasizing:

- Bullets do not magically support or prove anything. They are not a substitute for necessary description, analysis, and interpretation, and they do not replace the evidence and reasoning you would ordinarily be expected to provide. Bullets simply grab and direct the readers' attention by saying, "Look at me." The text following the bullet is what matters.
- Bullets should be used judiciously. Over-bulleting is much like crying "wolf" and expecting your reader to keep paying attention. Bullets should neither highlight every paragraph nor serve as some sort of annoying design element adorning every paragraph. Whole paragraphs can be bulleted when they develop a larger idea or argument to which they are subordinate. In these cases, each bulleted paragraph functions much like an item in a list, but with more elaboration. This paragraph and the previous one illustrate the point.

Use numbers, not bullets, to indicate a ranking or sequence.

The *U.S. News and World Report* ranked these schools as having the top Executive MBA programs in 2011:

[WITHOUT PUNCTUATION]	[WITH PUNCTUATION]
1. University of Pennsylvania	1. University of Pennsylvania,
2. University of Chicago	2. University of Chicago, and
3. Northwestern University	3. Northwestern University.

To assemble this product, follow these steps:

1. connect part A to part B	1. Connect part A to part B.
2. connect part B to part C	2. Connect part B to part C.
3. connect part C to part D	3. Connect part C to part D.

Use numbers instead of bullets for lengthy lists, even if the items are equal, because numbers allow for easier referencing. You would say, *Question 17 restates Question 4*, not *The seventeenth bulleted question restates the fourth bulleted question.* Use numbers also when you want to mark text *within* a paragraph, where bullets would not work because they must be vertically positioned to achieve their visual effect.

Choose a Typeface

Formatting your message also means choosing an appropriate typeface. Typefaces fall into two major categories: serif and sans-serif. Serif typefaces feature serifs, small, tail-like finishing touches on the ends of characters. San-serif typefaces do not have serifs. Popular serif typefaces include Baskerville Old Face, **Bookman Old Style**, Century, Garamond, Georgia, Palatino Linotype, and Times New Roman. Popular sans-serif typefaces include Arial, Calibri, Helvetica, Tahoma, and Verdana. (Typefaces shown are in 12-point type.)

Conventional wisdom, supported generally but not conclusively by several research studies, suggests that serif typefaces are easier to read than sans-serif typefaces in printed (hardcopy) text, which accounts for serif's widespread use in printed newspapers, magazines, and books. Sans-serif typefaces, though, are usually easier to read on a computer screen owing to the screen's lower resolution compared to the printed page. In print, sans-serif works best for headings and short copy, such as PowerPoint-type presentations, where each slide contains but a few lines of text.

Oddly, many writers choose sans-serif typefaces, like Arial, for their printed texts. In the absence of stronger evidence that sans-serif typefaces are as readable as serif typefaces in this format, it is wiser to stick with the latter. As we become more accustomed to sans-serif typefaces because of their widespread use in digital formats, we may eventually find sans-serif typefaces easier and faster to read in all formats. For now, however, serif typefaces should be your first choice for printed text. The problem of some serif typefaces appearing smaller and "muddier" can be rectified by increasing their point size from 12 to 12.5. When you do this with Times New Roman, for example, it appears similar in size to 12 point Arial.

- Times New Roman (12 point) versus Arial (12 point)
- Times New Roman (12.5 point) versus Arial (12 point)

Whatever typeface you choose should be well designed for its intended medium. Fortunately, new serif and sans-serif typefaces are continually being developed and improved specifically for the computer screen and the printed page.

RENO TIP **4.3**

RENOVATION TIP

When time allows, let another set of eyes review your writing. Friends and colleagues, even those having modest writing skills, can make excellent suggestions because it is easier to edit someone else's work than to compose your own. Take advantage of this fact and the help your friends and colleagues can provide.

Chapter 4

EXERCISES

EXERCISE 1. Revise these purpose statements to ensure they address one central thought expressed in a specific and precise declarative sentence that is confidently worded but not overly detailed.

A. Social networking sites may possibly have caused more harm than good.

B. This paper is about economic recessions.

C. What are the advantages of knowing Latin?

D. This tutorial explains how to register for general education courses, which can be taken as on-ground courses offered in fall and spring semesters, as well as in the winter intersession and summer session; as online courses offered in fall and spring semesters; and as hybrid courses, offered mostly in spring semester.

E. We should consider the possibility of lowering the unfair and hypocritical national minimum drinking age to 18.

F. Should our college ban alcohol on campus?

G. This report traces the causes of plagiarism and classroom incivility on college campuses.

H. Some action should be taken relative to the use of cell phones in public places.

I. Our college should provide more financial aid opportunities and tutoring services to students.

J. I am qualified for your advertised entry-level position in Public Relations because of my education, which includes a soon-to-be-earned BA in Public Relations from one of the top schools in the country, where I took several courses in PR theory and PR writing, as well as courses in persuasion, organizational communication, global communication, crisis management, and social media networking, while earning a 3.95 GPA (the only two B's I got were in GE courses), and because I have completed four internships in public relations—two with PR firms, one in the PR department of a large company, and one with a nonprofit agency; I also worked part-time with a start-up PR firm that gave me two raises in the four months I was there.

EXERCISE 2. Choose the purpose statement (A, B, C, or D) the other sentences (reasons) support.

1.
A. Bill is our top-performing employee.
B. The company should give Bill a raise.
C. If we don't reward Bill adequately, he will probably leave for another job.
D. Bill's work product exceeds his official job duties.

2.
A. The meal was inexpensive.
B. The meal was tasty.
C. The meal was healthy.
D. The meal was great.

3.
A. The Wildcats have the best coach in the league.
B. The Wildcats are experienced in winning.
C. The Wildcats will win the league championship.
D. The Wildcats have the best players in the league.

4.
A. The American Popular Culture course had five exams.
B. The American Popular Culture course was challenging.

C. The American Popular Culture course required five papers.
D. The American Popular Culture course discussed seven books.

5.
  A. The Office of Productivity is managed inefficiently.
  B. The Office of Productivity is overstaffed.
  C. The Office of Productivity is disorganized.
  D. The Office of Productivity offers services that duplicate one another.

EXERCISE 3. Organizing a clothes closet can help you develop the skills needed to organize a written message. Both the clothes closet and the written message must be structured into main categories (piles) and subordinate categories (sub-piles) to allow for easy access. Chart how you would organize the ideal clothes closet. Begin by grouping your shirts, pants, suits, sweaters, jackets, and shoes into categories. Then divide each of these main categories into as many subordinate categories as needed. Shirts, for example, can be separated by whether they are dress or casual style, followed by sleeve length (long or short), color, and fabric.

EXERCISE 4. Bring to class a term paper you are working on or have recently completed. Exchange papers with a classmate. Read your classmate's paper and then reverse outline its main ideas or main arguments, subideas or subarguments, and support material. Discuss whether your message and your classmate's message, as reflected by their reverse outlines, are organized effectively. Are any of the main ideas or main arguments, subideas or subarguments, and support materials out of place? What might be added, deleted, or revised to make the messages more compelling?

EXERCISE 5. Bring to class a lengthy newspaper, magazine, or Web-based article that has not been formatted with headings and subheadings. Exchange selections with a classmate. Format your classmate's selection with headings and, where appropriate, subheadings. Review and discuss how each of you made your formatting decisions. Are all your headings and subheadings needed? Are any others needed? Do your headings and subheadings effectively summarize the sections they cover? Could any be better worded?

5 Fortifying Sentences, Paragraphs, and Pages

The previous chapter discussed how to state your purpose, structure your ideas and arguments, and format your message. This chapter examines more ways to create effective paragraphs and pages. It discusses the need to analyze your specific audience and adapt your message to make it audience appealing; shows how to shepherd your sentences into unified, coherent paragraphs and pages that bolster your purpose; and explores various strategic choices for conceptualizing and organizing your message.

CHECK OUT YOUR AUDIENCE

Understanding your audience's beliefs and attitudes allows you to forge a stronger, more compelling message. This does not mean speaking out of both sides of your mouth, saying one thing to one audience and the opposite to another. It is your arguments, evidence, and language choices—not your principles—that you tailor to your specific audience. After you have gathered all your materials that support your case, you strategically decide which will most appeal to your specific audience.

The job application letter provides a good example. Its editorial demands reflect the importance of developing your *rhetorical literacy*: the ability to analyze your audience's needs and wants and then adapt accordingly. To create a well-adapted message, you must first put yourself in your readers' place by asking, What do my readers—not me, but *my readers*—need and want, and given what they need and want, how do I craft a satisfying message?

For most job application letters, it is crucial to show how your education, skills, and experience would benefit your potential employer. Job applicants, however, often make the mistake of stressing the valuable experience *they* would gain if hired. They write sentences like this: *I would love to work for your company because it would enable me to learn from some of the top professionals in the field as I prepare for a career in . . .* Asking an employer to serve as your personal trainer so you can develop your job skills (and move on to a better job?) is not exactly adapting to your audience's needs.

Readers are more willing to accept new ideas, such as hiring you, when they are linked to older, more acceptable ideas (i.e., bright, hardworking employees have always served this company well). Knowing something about your audience enables you to employ the power of analogy. Like the good teacher who relates new ideas to what students already know, good writers do the same.

Most job application letters, especially from recent college graduates, seem to be a combination of mush and bravado. It is a wonder anyone ever gets hired. First comes the mush. *Ever since I can remember—I think I was maybe 6 or 7 at the time—I've wanted to become an accountant. It's all I ever wanted to do. It's my dream job.* Who isn't passionate about one's career choice when just starting out and eagerly searching for a job? It is not something that separates you from the crowd or provides a compelling reason why you should be hired. Besides, being passionate does not necessarily mean you are any good.

More mush:

- No one will work harder than I will.

  Talk about bold moves to distance yourself from all those other applicants who said they were lazy.

- It would be an honor and a privilege to work for an industry-leading company such as yours.

  This sort of obsequious drivel again makes the strategic error of focusing on you and how you, not the company, would benefit from your hiring. The implication is that once you have some experience, you will be in a position to move on to another, better job. This is like using *first marriage* to describe one still in progress.

A good application letter focuses on two key questions: How would the employer benefit by hiring me? And what evidence can I give to support my case?

In most job listings, employers place strong communication skills at the top of their job qualifications. Applicants usually respond, *I have very strong communication skills.* By itself, this does not mean much, given no one expects to hear the reverse, *I communicate poorly and always have, but I thought I'd apply anyway.* If you say you communicate well, you need to provide a credible, evidence-based rationale.

Application letters often proclaim expertise, if not greatness, usually with a string of sentences all starting with I. *I have terrific interpersonal skills and I am an excellent team player. I excel in meeting deadlines. I am the best at multitasking. I am exceptionally conscientious.* The writer is also fabulous at withholding any evidence that would support these assertions.

The challenge of any application letter is to highlight all your skills and accomplishments in a way that does not make you sound like a braggart.

One way of extolling your virtues while maintaining your likability is to let the facts speak for themselves. It is better to write, *I honed my communication skills by working three years in customer service* than *I shrewdly added to my already incredible communication abilities by devoting myself to working three demanding years in customer service, where I was awesome.*

An argument is a conclusion supported by evidence and reasoning. The test of whether you are making an effective argument in your application letter, and in general, is twofold: Does your audience perceive your argument to be relevant to your purpose? Does your audience perceive your argument to be supported by sound evidence (sufficient in quality and quantity) and reasoning? An effective argument meets both criteria.

Let's assume your application letter gives these arguments why the employer should hire you (your purpose): *I am well trained for the position, possess strong communication skills, strive to be a team player, and have committed myself to saving the planet.* To win over any prospective employer, these arguments must be seen as germane. If your reader views your commitment to save the planet as irrelevant to job performance, the argument becomes moot and should not be made.

On the other hand, if your prospective employer sees a commitment to saving the planet as central to your job duties, you *would* want to argue you are so committed, provided you can make the case convincingly. But if your evidence is lacking, you will unlikely persuade your reader, and you may lose credibility. This loss in credibility can affect how your audience perceives *all* your arguments. Suddenly, even your well-evidenced arguments may be looked upon differently and reevaluated less favorably because you are now perceived as less credible. This is particularly true in cases where you argue strongly against something or someone, as in the example in Chapter 4, *Roger should be fired because he is emotionally unstable.* When you make such an argument without much evidence, it lowers your credibility because you are seen as attacking without sufficient cause. A badly supported argument is worse than none at all.

Some writers will knowingly advance a weak argument, hoping it may have some appeal. They think that a weak argument, at most, will not be accepted as support for their purpose and will just be ignored. The larger harm of weak arguments is that they are *not* ignored. Rather, they are processed as a sign of the writer's intelligence and character. They affect the reader's overall perception of whether the writer is credible and to what extent the reader should believe anything the writer says.

Whether you are writing an application letter or any other message, the amount of evidence you provide for your arguments depends on whom you are addressing. If your readers initially agree with you, much less evidence is required than if they are undecided or opposed to your position. Provide your readers with all the evidence they need to be persuaded, but do not waste time evidencing arguments they already accept. Better yet, why waste time even making such arguments? After all, do you really need to convince your prospective employer you want the job, respect the company, and would relish the opportunity to prove yourself?

SHEPHERD YOUR SENTENCES

Rally Around the Topic Sentence

A paragraph is a unit of composition that supports your purpose statement. Generally, a paragraph (excluding your paragraphs of introduction and conclusion) establishes one main idea or main argument summarized by your topic sentence, normally the paragraph's first sentence, and developed, directly or indirectly, by the rest of the paragraph. The topic sentence is your promise of what your readers will find in the paragraph. When you do not follow through with this pledge—when your paragraph does not develop its topic sentence or when it includes material not on point—your readers are led astray.

Not every paragraph must begin with a topic sentence. When a long paragraph is broken into two or more paragraphs to make it easier to read, the second and subsequent paragraphs can continue to develop the topic sentence introduced in the first paragraph. You do not need to formally reintroduce your topic sentence, although you may want to remind your reader of the paragraph's purpose as you start your second or third new paragraph. *Another example of how Roger lies is . . .*

It is customary not to have topic sentences when writing in narrative form. Topic sentences here would halt the flow and drama of the story. The narrative style is central to fiction, but it appears less in business writing and academic writing, which stress a more overt structuring and labeling of main ideas and main arguments.

A descriptive paragraph may not require a topic sentence if its purpose is apparent. If you were to describe the facial features of a friend, for example, you would likely start with one feature and then move to the next. Your reader would almost immediately know what you were doing. You would not need a topic sentence, such as *I will describe the facial features of my friend*. In persuasive messages, the absence of topic sentences is unusual, although you may occasionally conclude that your argument is so evident throughout the paragraph that a topic sentence would come across as clumsy overkill.

Another reason for not employing a topic sentence is when you decide that the paragraph's main idea or main argument will have more impact if the reader, not you, completes it. To effectively execute this decision, you must be a first-rate writer capable of holding your readers' attention while nimbly steering toward the paragraph's main idea or main argument. Of course, your readers face the disadvantage of starting the paragraph without an immediate sense of where it is going.

You may choose to place a topic sentence somewhere other than at the top of the paragraph. Should you perceive your paragraph's main idea or main argument to be so off-putting to readers that it stands a better chance of acceptance if it comes after you have presented its supporting evidence, you can adopt a climactic approach (discussed in Chapter 4), where you conclude the paragraph with your topic sentence. It is more often the writer's tone, however—not the decision to start with a controversial idea or argument—that alienates audiences.

Writers sometimes delay introducing a topic sentence because they want to first "set the stage" for what follows. They lead with a transitional statement or an internal summary or both, followed by the topic sentence. For example:

¶ *If you thought that being a dishonest and poor manager were not enough justification to fire Roger, think again. The most pressing reason for firing him is his emotional instability.*

Frequently, transitions and internal summaries can be combined into the topic sentence. *Besides being a dishonest and poor manager, the most pressing reason Roger should be fired is that he is emotionally unstable.* Time and again, however, writers waste paragraph beginnings on obvious, unnecesary statements before getting to the topic sentence. *Now I will discuss the issue of emotional stability. Roger is emotionally unstable.*

A good topic sentence makes the paragraph not only easier to read and remember, but also easier to write. Think of it as a mantra (metaphor option 1) that guides your efforts and keeps you focused. Even when it stays in your head and never makes the page, the topic sentence controls everything you do in the paragraph. It is the anchor (metaphor option 2) around which you tie your thoughts to keep them from drifting off. Whether you explicitly state your topic sentence or whether it implicitly resides in your text, it directs what you say and how you say it.

When you first compose your topic sentence, consider it a "working," or tentative, version that you may need to revise once you have completed the paragraph and can view all your sentences at once. Questions similar to those you would ask when developing your purpose statement (discussed in Chapter 4) can help you evaluate your topic sentence: Does every sentence in the paragraph either directly support the topic sentence or shore up other sentences that support the topic sentence? If not, should I revise my topic sentence to encompass all the sentences that follow? Or would it be better to revise, delete, or add sentences to bring the paragraph in line with my topic sentence? Or must I fix both my topic sentence and one or more sentences that follow? Your goal is to create a unified paragraph, where all the sentences come together in common cause to support your topic sentence.

One way of identifying which sentences do not belong in the paragraph is by determining whether each sentence answers the same basic question the topic sentence would if it were turned into a question. For example, *Roger is emotionally unstable* answers the question, Is Roger emotionally stable? All sentences in the paragraph must address this question in some way. When they do not, they should be revised, deleted, or moved elsewhere in the message under topic sentences they do support.

What most writers find much tougher to delete are eloquent sentences not on point. A sentence, regardless how stellar, must still speak to the message at hand. In *Style: Toward Clarity and Grace*, Joseph M. Williams observes: "There is more to readable writing than local clarity. A series of clear sentences can still be confusing if we fail to design them to fit their context, to reflect a consistent point of view, to emphasize our most important ideas." We become so enamored with our own words that we hesitate to part with any of them. Seasoned writers, though, have no such problem. They stay focused on their purpose, and they know that every word must support their purpose. Example 5.1 embellishes Lincoln's Gettysburg Address to include famous portions of other speeches. Which sentences do not belong?

5.1 Student Example

Four score and seven years ago our fathers brought forth on this continent, a new nation, conceived in Liberty, and dedicated to the proposition that all men are created equal. We hold these truths to be self-evident, that all men are created equal, that they are endowed by their Creator with certain unalienable rights, that among these are life, liberty and the pursuit of happiness.

The future doesn't belong to the fainthearted; it belongs to the brave. Now we are engaged in a great civil war, testing whether that nation, or any nation so conceived and so dedicated, can long endure. We are met on a great battlefield of that war. We have come to dedicate a portion of that field, as a final resting place for those who here gave their lives that that nation might live. It is altogether fitting and proper that we should do this. The only thing we have to fear is fear itself.

But, in a larger sense, we cannot dedicate—we cannot consecrate—we cannot hallow—this ground. I have nothing to offer but blood, toil, tears, and sweat. The brave men, living and dead, who struggled here, have consecrated it, far above our poor power to add or detract. The world will little note, nor long remember what we say here, but it can never forget what they did here. Let every nation know, whether it wishes us well or ill, that we shall pay any price, bear any burden, meet any hardship, support any friend, oppose any foe, to assure the survival and the success of liberty.

It is for us the living, rather, to be dedicated here to the unfinished work which they who fought here have thus far so nobly advanced. It is rather for us to be here dedicated to the great task remaining before us—that from these honored dead we take increased devotion to that cause for which they gave the last full measure of devotion—that we here highly resolve that these dead shall not have died in vain—that this nation, under God, shall have a new birth of freedom—and that government of the people, by the people, for the people, shall not perish from the earth.

The italicized text in Example 5.2 is from (1) The Declaration of Independence, 1776; (2) Ronald Reagan's Address to the Nation on the Challenger Space Shuttle Disaster, 1986; (3) Franklyn Delano Roosevelt's First Inaugural Address, 1932; (4) Winston Churchill's first speech before the House of Commons after being appointed Prime Minister, 1940; and (5) John F. Kennedy's Inaugural Address, 1961. As you read through this version again, note how each of these added passages moves the text away from Lincoln's purpose—a promise to renew the nation's commitment to freedom, equality, and democracy—and how they break the unity of Lincoln's message.

5.2   Student Example

Four score and seven years ago our fathers brought forth on this continent, a new nation, conceived in Liberty, and dedicated to the proposition that all men are created equal. [1] *We hold these truths to be self-evident, that all men are created equal, that they are endowed by their Creator with certain unalienable rights, that among these are life, liberty and the pursuit of happiness.*

[2] *The future doesn't belong to the fainthearted; it belongs to the brave.* Now we are engaged in a great civil war, testing whether that nation, or any nation so conceived and so dedicated, can long endure. We are met on a great battlefield of that war. We have come to dedicate a portion of that field, as a final resting place for those who here gave their lives that that nation might live. It is altogether fitting and proper that we should do this. [3] *The only thing we have to fear is fear itself.*

But, in a larger sense, we cannot dedicate—we cannot consecrate—we cannot hallow—this ground. [4] *I have nothing to offer but blood, toil, tears, and sweat.* The brave men, living and dead, who struggled here, have consecrated it, far above our poor power to add or detract. The world will little note, nor long remember what we say here, but it can never forget what they did here. [5] *Let every nation know, whether it wishes us well or ill, that we shall pay any price, bear any burden, meet any hardship, support any friend, oppose any foe, to assure the survival and the success of liberty.*

It is for us the living, rather, to be dedicated here to the unfinished work which they who fought here have thus far so nobly advanced. It is rather for us to be here dedicated to the great task remaining before us—that from these honored dead we take increased devotion to that cause for which they gave the last full measure of devotion—that we here highly resolve that these dead shall not have died in vain—that this nation, under God, shall have a new birth of freedom—and that government of the people, by the people, for the people, shall not perish from the earth.

RENO TIP   5.1

RENOVATION TIP

Imagine your paragraph as a herd of cattle (your sentences), with you as the ever-vigilant cowhand (writer) charged with rounding up the herd and keeping it together. Cattle that drift off must be brought back to the herd (the paragraph), while those having strayed from other herds (other paragraphs) must be returned. By checking the brand (determining how each sentence is implicitly labeled by the topic sentence it supports), you can identify where the cattle belong.

Worry Not About Length

Theoretically, a paragraph can be any length; there is no minimum or maximum word requirement. But exceptionally long paragraphs, even when devoted to one main idea or main argument, can be challenging to read because they do not provide any visual break in the form of white space that permits readers to pause, catch their breath, and mentally refresh. Although long paragraphs may require breaking, short paragraphs do not warrant expanding just because they are short. A paragraph should be as long as necessary to sufficiently develop its main idea or main argument.

In daily journalism, news stories, feature stories, in-depth pieces, and editorials frequently employ one- and two-sentence paragraphs. This makes sense given the nature of the journalistic form, which, in contrast to other literary genres, tends to abstract main ideas and main arguments. The convention of short paragraphs in journalism grew out of the need to conform to the traditional layout of newspapers (narrow columns), where long paragraphs would be even harder to read, and the need to easily cut copy, which short paragraphs facilitated. In today's digital journalism, which places a premium on the speed of story production, short paragraphs, insofar as they compartmentalize thought, allow for quicker editorial decisions about what to keep and what to cut.

In more formal writing, such as academic papers, which is often thesis driven, one-sentence paragraphs are less prevalent. This is not because of some minimum-length requirement everyone has secretly adopted. Rather, one- and two-sentence paragraphs are rare because the development of a paragraph's main idea or main argument typically requires more than one or two sentences. The short paragraph usually is defective not because it is short per se, but because it is undeveloped. Still, you will find instances of one- and two-sentence paragraphs even in the best academic writing. They often appear in the form of a preview sentence that introduces an idea or argument having multiple parts.

> Beyond its commercial success and critical acclaim—winning seven Academy Awards, including top honors for Best Picture, Best Director, and Best Actor—*The Bridge on River Kwai* remains a haunting experience because of its intriguing characters and unique plot, its multiple and constantly shifting perspectives, and, of course, its somewhat ambiguous ending. [Subsequent paragraphs develop these themes.]

The one-sentence paragraph is also effective for emphasizing contradiction, contrast, and irony. After spending a paragraph listing all the promises the governor made upon taking office, you follow with this one-sentence paragraph: *Four years later, none of these promises have been fulfilled.* After spending a paragraph describing the glamorous lifestyle of a star professional basketball player, you follow with this one-sentence paragraph: *Meanwhile, most of his former teammates are back living at home, unemployed, and looking for a break.* After spending a paragraph describing how you study all the time while your girlfriend never even fakes opening a book, you follow with this one-sentence paragraph: *Yet, incredibly, my girlfriend is seen as a potential Rhodes Scholar.*

Smooth the Rough Edges

Whatever the length of a paragraph, it must be coherent: Sentences should follow one another logically and linguistically. They should connect so effortlessly that readers begin to anticipate what will come next. Developing a good topic sentence and building upon it carefully (discussed earlier in this chapter), along with organizing your ideas or arguments effectively (discussed in Chapter 4), can go a long way in securing coherent paragraphs.

It is useful to continually ask, What can I add, delete, rewrite, or reposition to improve coherence and create a wave-like effect where each sentence in the paragraph naturally leads into another? In the following example, the paragraph is unified insofar as everything supports the topic sentence, but the paragraph lacks coherence because no linkage is drawn between the sentences, some of which are also out of place. The result is a paragraph whose sentences do not play together as a team.

ORIGINAL   The university will require all students to take three, two-unit physical activity courses. Next fall will be when it will take place. Denunciation best describes the immediate reaction of students when they heard about this. The fact that students should not be required by the university to play games was the major student complaint. There are exceptions: Students over 35 and veterans who have returned from military combat will be exempt. The activity courses will replace six units of current General Education requirements. Exemption requests from computer jocks will be handled on a case-by-case basis. Students having senior standing in the fall do not need to worry because they are also exempt from the new requirement.

To underscore the incoherence of this paragraph, let's put the sentences into a list before revising them:

1. The university will require all students to take three, two-unit physical activity courses.
2. Next fall will be when it will take place.
3. Denunciation best describes the immediate reaction of students when they heard about this.
4. The fact that students should not be required by the university to play games was the major student complaint.
5. There are exceptions: Students over 35 and veterans who have returned from military combat will be exempt.
6. The activity courses will replace six units of current General Education requirements.
7. Exemption requests from computer jocks will be handled on a case-by-case basis.
8. Students having senior standing in the fall do not need to worry because they are also exempt from the new requirement.

Now, let's revise these sentences:

EFFECTIVE NEXT FALL,
1. ~~The~~ university will require all students to take three, two-unit physical activity courses.

2. ~~Next fall will be when it will take place.~~

IMMEDIATELY, STUDENTS DENOUNCED THE NEW POLICY.
3. ~~Denunciation best describes the immediate reaction of students when they heard about this.~~

THEY COMPLAINED THEY
4. ~~The fact that students~~ should not be required by the university to play games. ~~was the major student complaint.~~

SOME OF THESE   HOWEVER, WILL BE EXEMPTED, INCLUDING THOSE
5. ~~These are exceptions.~~ Students, over 35, ~~and~~ veterans who have returned from military combat, ~~will be exempt.~~

2.   SE
~~5.~~ The activity courses will replace six units of current General Education requirements.

(MOVE UP
TO BECOME
2ND SENT.)
6.
~~7.~~ Exemption requests from computer jocks will be handled on a case-by-case basis.

AND THOSE
~~8.~~ ~~Students~~ having senior standing in the fall. ~~do not need to worry because they are also exempt from the new requirement.~~

The final, paragraph version:

REVISION   Effective next fall, the university will require all students to take three, two-unit physical activity courses. These activity courses will replace six units of current General Education requirements. Immediately, students denounced the new policy. They complained they should not be required by the university to play games. Some of these students, however, will be exempted, including those over 35, veterans who have returned from military combat, and those having senior standing in the fall. Exemption requests from computer jocks will be handled on a case-by-case basis.

The lack of paragraph coherence is what usually betrays the student plagiarist. Long before turnitin.com and other similar-type services were available, faculty had little difficulty detecting plagiarized papers. It was not just what the student stole that alerted the professor, but, rather, what the student wrote alongside the lifted material. The inconsistency of the two styles—one having a coherence characterized by elegant, intertwined sentences skillfully punctuated; the other defined by awkwardly worded, oddly sequenced sentences poorly punctuated—revealed the presence of either two writers or one multiple-personality author. Faculty chose to believe it was the former.

Contributing mightily to the problem of incoherence is the awkwardly worded sentence, which often results from a lack of parallel sentence structure. Unparallel constructions distort not just the rhythm but also the sense of the sentence. They make it harder to quickly see how all the elements in the sentence cohere. In the story that follows, the grammatical structure of the original sentence changes and becomes internally inconsistent. The revised version corrects the offending grammatical structure, putting it in harmony with the rest of the sentence.

ORIGINAL	Yvone was attracted to Wayne because he excelled at singing, dancing, and had very good knowledge about how to write.
REVISION	Yvone was attracted to Wayne because he excelled at singing, dancing, and writing.
ORIGINAL	Wayne was attracted to Yvone because she wrote best-selling novels, spoke five languages, was someone who loved fine chocolate, and had ownership of an online editing service.
REVISION	Wayne was attracted to Yvone because she wrote best-selling novels, spoke five languages, loved fine chocolate, and owned an online editing service.
ORIGINAL	Although he was interested in Yvone, Wayne also faced mounting punctuation problems with his latest manuscript, so he pondered, Should I date her or be hiring her? Or would it be just easier to forget her than asking her out?
REVISION	Although he was interested in Yvone, Wayne also faced mounting punctuation problems with his latest manuscript, so he pondered, Should I date her or hire her? Or would it be just as easy to forget her than to ask her out?
ORIGINAL	Meanwhile, Yvone wondered whether Wayne was uninterested in her or his work preoccupied him.
REVISION	Meanwhile, Yvone wondered whether Wayne was uninterested in her or whether he was preoccupied with his work.
ORIGINAL	Yvone decided she would take matters into her own hands and invite Wayne to either a picnic at the park or have lunch at the beach.
REVISION	Yvone decided she would take things into her own hands and invite Wayne to either a picnic at the park or a lunch at the beach.

ORIGINAL	Simultaneously, Wayne had an epiphany: Not experiencing love would be worse than if you had the experience but then lost it.
REVISION	Simultaneously, Wayne had an epiphany: It would be better to have loved and lost than never to have loved at all.

You can also achieve paragraph (and page) coherence by providing cues that aid readers to see what you are doing and where you are going. Some suggestions:

LABEL (LINGUISTICALLY IDENTIFY) YOUR PURPOSE.   *I contend . . . , I propose . . . , My purpose is . . . , This e-mail outlines . . . , This report describes . . . ,* or *This paper argues . . .* help to identify your purpose. Labeling your purpose ensures you will actually have one. In informal writing, where liberal formatting is more acceptable, writers will sometimes italicize or boldface their purpose statement.

LABEL YOUR IDEAS OR ARGUMENTS.   *Foremost, Roger should be fired because . . . , Another reason why Roger should be fired . . . ,* or *Too, Roger . . .* are examples of how you can label your ideas or arguments. Other words you can use to signal the introduction of a new idea or argument include *additionally, and, also, besides, beyond, further, furthermore, in addition, likewise,* and *moreover.* You can also label ideas or arguments using *first, second,* and *third,* or choose to mark them numerically or alphabetically: *1, 2, 3; (a), (b), (c).* Again, in more informal writing, you can italicize, boldface, or bullet each of your main ideas or main arguments.

LABEL YOUR COMPARISONS, CONTRASTS, AND CONNECTIONS.   Readers will follow your message more easily if you reinforce important comparisons, contrasts, and connections with transitions, such as *although . . . , as opposed to . . . , identical to . . . , in contrast to . . . , however . . . , meanwhile . . . , much like . . . , on the other hand . . . , rather than . . . , similarly . . . , so too . . . , whereas . . . ,* or *yet . . .* You can also emphasize the connection between your ideas or arguments by using bridging phrases and words, such as *accordingly, as a result, as such, consequently, hence, so, that is why, therefore,* and *thus.*

LABEL AND SUMMARIZE KEY PARTS OF YOUR MESSAGE.   You can label summary-type sentences with *finally . . . , generally . . . , in brief . . . , in conclusion . . . , in other words . . . , in short . . . , in sum . . . , in summary . . . , last . . . ,* or *overall . . .*

It is helpful, particularly at the end of longer messages, to remind readers of your purpose and your main ideas or main arguments. Restating them in your conclusion drives home your message. You can also summarize at the beginning of your message with a preview, as well as in middle of your message with an internal summary. If your message is short enough, a summary is not needed.

Overestimating their audience's ability to follow and retain message content, some writers give short shrift to labeling and summarizing. They know their message so well they are unaware just how much they subvocalize their thoughts. They fail to realize that even a well-organized message, let alone one with gaps, can be harder to follow when labels and summaries are missing.

Others believe that labeling and summarizing will come across as speaking down to their audience. But it is never clarity that audiences resent; it is arrogance, smugness, and deception. Readers welcome writers who take the extra steps to ensure comprehension of their messages. No one ever complains, *The message was much too easy to follow for my tastes. I prefer when it's more confusing.*

RENO
TIP   **5.2**

RENOVATION TIP

To assess whether you have written a unified and coherent paragraph, randomly rearrange the paragraph's sentences and ask a classmate to reassemble them. Does the classmate's reassembled paragraph differ from yours? What would your classmate edit, delete, or add to give the paragraph more unity and coherence? You can use this same approach to test the larger organization of your paper. Select any series of paragraphs, reorder them randomly, and observe how someone else would sequence and revise them.

STRATEGIZE YOUR CASE

The nature of your content favors certain strategic choices and organizational patterns over others. Making the best decisions depends on knowing what your purpose statement entails and what you must prove to gain its acceptance.

From the discipline of Communication/Communication Studies come useful lessons on how to categorize and organize messages strategically. Disciplinary courses in public speaking and argumentation conceptualize informative and persuasive speeches in ways that can also be broadly applied to informative and persuasive written messages. Just as the speaker's purpose dictates message strategy, so, too, does the writer's purpose.

The categories delineated here serve as a guide, not as hard-and-fast rules, for constructing texts that sway readers. They are presented in the context of how they might be generalized to written messages. They will require additional adaptation depending on the requirements of specific writing assignments.

Strategize Persuasive Messages

Before you write any persuasive message, determine whether you are advocating a **proposition of fact**, **proposition of value**, or **proposition of policy**.

A **proposition of fact** proposes that something was/was not, is/is not, or will/will not be true. It does not make any value judgment about the truth, nor does it recommend any course of action in light of it. When you argue a proposition of fact, you ask your audience to accept or reject a "larger" factual conclusion based on your presentation of "smaller" supportive facts. Agreed-upon facts—for example, the sun rises in the east and sets in the west, George Washington was the first president of the United States, or Maine is north of

Florida—do not lend themselves to debate. Arguable propositions of fact on which we disagree are another matter. *The dinosaurs were killed by a meteor shower. Childhood vaccines do not cause autism. The rate of inflation will decrease next year.*

Propositions of fact dominate criminal courtroom proceedings. The prosecution, for example, claims that Ralph committed the murder (big fact), as evidenced by several smaller facts: He threatened several times to kill the victim, he was seen arguing with the victim just before gunshots were heard, he fled the country immediately after the crime, gunpowder residue was found on his hands, his fingerprints were on the gun that killed the victim, his clothes were splattered with the victim's blood, an eyewitness saw him shoot the victim, and he bragged on his Facebook account about killing the victim.

Most propositions of fact can be organized in one of two ways:

1. When you argue that something is true because it meets the criteria, or exhibits the qualities, that define it as true, you are using a *definitional criteria* design. Take this example: *Many first-year college students lack essential writing skills.* To support this proposition, you must directly or indirectly reference what you mean by "essential writing skills." Often your arguments will indirectly reference your defining criteria. Note how the writer's implicit criteria (italicized) compose part of each main argument in these sentences:

- Many first-year college students do not know *how to choose a thesis.*
- Many first-year college students do not know *how to organize ideas and arguments.*
- Many first-year college students do not know *how to write grammatically correct sentences.*

Sometimes your audience may not accept your implied definitional criteria. They may not see why choosing a thesis, organizing ideas and arguments, and knowing grammar constitute essential writing skills. For this audience, you would need to directly state and justify your criteria before applying it. Your second paragraph following your introduction might begin by saying, *Essential writing skills include knowing how to choose a thesis, organize ideas and arguments, and write grammatically correct sentences.* After defending these criteria, you would move on to why first-year students do not meet the standard.

2. When you argue that one fact causes another fact, you are using a *causal* design. If you were to contend that *The lack of essential writing skills leads to lower grades*, you would be saying that one (established) fact, the lack of essential writing skills, causes another fact (the effect): professors giving lower grades to students. You do not need to argue that students lack essential writing skills, but you must show that the lack of those skills would cause lower grades. The body of your message might develop these arguments:

- A student's lack of essential writing skills prevents a professor from fully understanding what the student is saying.
- A student's lack of essential writing skills lowers a professor's perception of the student's knowledge.
- A student's lack of essential writing skills lowers a professor's perception of the student's intelligence.

A causal design differs from a causal argument. Messages organized around a causal design have as their overall purpose to establish a causal relationship, reflected in the message's statement of purpose, such as *The lack of essential writing skills leads to lower grades.* In this example, the purpose statement is also supported with causal arguments. Causal arguments may be used to support propositions of fact, value, and policy, and they can also support informative messages.

A **proposition of value** proposes the assigning of a specific value to an agreed-upon fact; it does not present any course of action relating to the value. Your value judgment is one of right or wrong, ethical or unethical, good or bad, fair or unfair. Or you may comparatively evaluate your subject, asserting that it is better, superior, nobler—or in some other way more worthy or less worthy—than something else. *Killing animals for food is immoral. It is unfair to give every student an A in the course regardless of his or her class performance. The negative stereotyping of pit bulls is wrong.*

A proposition of value requires that you establish *evaluation criteria,* directly or indirectly, for judging your subject. Take this example: *Dogs make better pets than cats.* (Cat lovers, of course, will want to argue the reverse.) The agreed-upon facts are that dogs, cats, and pets all exist. That is not so, for instance, of extraterrestrials. To argue that dogs make better pets than extraterrestrials would necessitate suspending the debate until first settling a proposition of fact: *Extraterrestrials exist.* If a proposition of value contains disputed words or terms, advocacy cannot go forward until the dispute is resolved.

In maintaining that dogs make better pets than cats, you could offer these arguments:

- Dogs are smarter than cats.
- Dogs are more loyal than cats.
- Dogs are more affectionate than cats.
- Dogs are more protective than cats.

To persuade your readers, you must first convince them that intelligence, loyalty, affection, and protection are valid criteria for determining a superior pet, or, more precisely, that these qualities should be valued over other qualities. Cat lovers will counter that your criteria are not valid or that they are incomplete because they do not include such traits as independence and self-sufficiency; nor do your criteria, they will say, take into account that cats catch mice, groom themselves, and do not bark. Because cat lovers are unlikely to accept your criteria, convincing them that dogs make better pets than cats will prove elusive no matter how strong your evidence that dogs are more intelligent, loyal, affectionate, and protective.

If your readers were to accept your criteria of what constitutes a superior pet, you would still need to show that dogs meet the criteria better than cats. One could contend that cats, not dogs, are smarter, more loyal, more affectionate, and more protective; or cats are smarter than dogs, and this quality alone outweighs the other three. Or your readers may integrate a portion of your criteria with a larger portion of their own and say that cats make better pets than dogs because they are smarter, more independent, and more self-sufficient. All of this suggests in the end it is probably best to own both a dog and a cat.

A **proposition of policy** proposes that a current policy should be changed or abolished or that some new policy should be adopted where there was none. A proposition of policy may also state that a policy should *not* be adopted. "Policy" broadly refers to the current state of affairs or how things operate now, which is called the *status quo*. An affirmatively worded proposition of policy (one without the word "not" in it) proposes an action that would alter the status quo. Propositions of policy usually contain the word *should*. *The sale and use of all alcoholic beverages should be prohibited. The terminally ill should be allowed to end their lives. The university should require all students to learn Greek.*

One way of organizing a proposition of policy is by following a *problem-solution* design. You present a significant problem with the status quo and then provide a solution. In practice, you reference the solution (either specifically or broadly) in your purpose statement, develop the problem and its causes, and then get back to your solution, which solves the problem.

Let's return to our now familiar purpose statement *Roger should be fired as CEO*. The purpose statement, which includes the solution, is followed by three arguments—*Roger is dishonest, Roger cannot manage,* and *Roger is emotionally unstable*—that address why Roger's presidency (the status quo) is problematic. When you advocate a major change in policy such as this, you must show that a problem exists and that it is *significant* enough to warrant the time, effort, and risk usually involved in making any major policy change.

The actual decision to fire Roger is not a complicated action that requires much, if any, detailed discussion on how it would be carried out. It suffices to restate the solution at the end of your message, reminding your reader that firing Roger would put an end to his flawed leadership.

In other cases, the solution and its implementation may require more discussion and justification, which would typically come after you have established the problem and the need for change. Again, your analysis of your purpose statement informs your strategic decisions about where you focus your message. Ask yourself, Assuming my readers agree there is a significant problem, would they support my solution? Or might they see other, better ways to solve the problem?

However compelling your indictment of the status quo, you must still provide an effective solution that does not incur other problems along the way. Readers should not be left to conclude:

- Yes, I agree we have a serious drug problem in America, but shooting drug users on the spot is not the best solution.
- Yes, homelessness is not a good thing, but shipping the homeless to Antarctica is absurd.
- Yes, the football team is awful, but abolishing the program goes too far.

Finding the right solution can be trickier than establishing the problem. Consider this proposition: *The university should adopt a more proactive policy for reducing student cheating*. First, you must establish that cheating is a serious problem. You could argue that it is rampant on campus, getting worse, and not being taken seriously enough by the school. These arguments would be introduced by similarly worded topic sentences heading the paragraphs that develop the arguments.

In presenting your solution, you would need to answer these questions: What do I mean by a "more proactive policy"? How will the new policy reduce cheating? Is the new policy doable? What would be the ramifications of adopting such a policy? One unique approach—granted, not the most compelling—would make these arguments:

- The university can reduce cheating by paying "student spotters" to report on other students who cheat. The program would be set up like this . . .
- Using "student spotters" will lead to more reported instances of cheating because students are in the best position to know what other students are doing. Students live together, eat together, study together . . .
- Many students will stop cheating once they realize there is a greater chance they will get caught. This has been shown by . . .
- The cost of this program, including paying students and setting up an on-campus Cheating Detection Office with a full-time director, would be $500,000 a year, which could be raised by adding a $25 annual "anti-cheaters fee" to the student activity fee.
- Although many naysayers would have you believe that students reporting on other students is an inane idea that would lead to a hostile, police-state environment, that is not true. First, the reporting process would be anonymous . . .

If your readers already agree with you about what is wrong with the status quo (for example, drug abuse is harmful, homelessness is bad, and the football team never wins), it is unnecessary to rehash the problem. The better strategy is to focus on how your proposed solution provides the best remedy.

Assume, for a moment, the company fires Roger, thanks in part to your well-articulated report outlining all his faults. It then announces it is looking for a new CEO and wants someone who can restore honesty, managerial competence, and emotional stability to its top leadership post. These job qualifications reflect what is missing from the company (the problem), which it hopes to fix by hiring a new CEO (solution). So who should the company hire?

In presenting your case for Neal, you do not need to reiterate that the company lacks an honest, managerially competent, emotionally stable leader; everyone already knows this. Instead, you must show that Neal represents the best solution.

After an introductory paragraph that includes your purpose statement, *Neal should be appointed CEO*, your reasons can be introduced with topic sentences, such as these:

- Neal would be an honest CEO.
- Equally important, Neal would effectively manage the company.
- Furthermore, Neal would bring emotional stability to the position.

In short, Neal is the strongest candidate for solving the company's needs (the problem).

Sometimes you may want to persuade your audience that the status quo should be changed not so much because a clear-cut problem exists, but because change would bring about significant advantages. In this design, called *comparative advantages*, you show how your proposed change would be comparatively advantageous over the status quo. For example, a friend tries to convince you to move to another apartment. She proposes that living in the new apartment would be comparatively advantageous to staying in your current apartment because the new place is bigger, nicer, pet friendlier, and much cheaper. Each advantage would be worded as an argument and introduced with topic sentences such as these:

- Moving to the new apartment would give you more space.
- This space would also be more luxurious.
- Buddy would benefit from the larger dog run in the new apartment.
- Best of all, rent for the new apartment is much less than what you now pay.

If you were to point out that these advantages identify needs not being met by the status quo and, thus, do reflect a problem with the status quo, you would be correct. In a comparative-advantages design as opposed to a problem-solution design, however, the focus remains on how and why the proposed change brings about significant advantages.

Strategize Informative Messages

When you present an informative message, you assume the role of teacher rather than advocate. Your primary intent is not to persuade your reader to accept an arguable truth, embrace a value, or take an action. Rather, your aim is to inform your audience by describing or explaining data about which it has little or no knowledge. Although the readers' processing of your information may subsequently affect their beliefs, attitudes, and behaviors, this is not your main purpose.

Informative purposes can sound similar to persuasive propositions of fact. The key difference is that a proposition of fact advances a partisan position on a debatable, usually controversial, question of fact. *What killed the dinosaurs? Do childhood vaccines cause autism? Will the rate of inflation increase next year?* An informative message answers a different kind of factual question, one that asks for a neutral presentation of generally accepted information. *What types of dinosaurs existed? What are the symptoms of autism? How does one measure the rate of inflation?*

Writers sometimes mischaracterize persuasive messages as informative. Using words associated with informative communication, they advance persuasive propositions under the guise of informing the reader. *This paper will* **describe** *how the earth was first populated by Martians* (proposition of fact). *I will* **discuss** *why cheating at solitaire is wrong* (proposition of value). *What follows is an* **explanation** *of why the Theatre Department's online acting courses should be* *dropped from the curriculum* (proposition of policy). It is misleading to label your purpose as informative when your intent is to persuade.

Writing an informative message is not necessarily easier than drafting a persuasive one. Each presents a different set of challenges. In a persuasive message, you try to move readers toward your position by finding and adapting arguments that appeal to their mindset. In an informative message, you seek to enlighten your audience by discussing information in ways that are relevant and interesting. Unlike persuasive texts whose subject matter often commands attention, informative texts address topics that sometimes have a tougher time drawing and sustaining reader interest. On the other hand, informative messages usually do not meet the resistance faced by many persuasive messages.

Informative messages can be organized in various ways, but the most common designs include *categorical, categorical comparative, causal, chronological/ sequential,* and *narrative.*

CATEGORICAL.   A categorical design breaks a topic into categories. If you were describing a theatrical play, for example, you could describe its character(s), setting, conflict, and resolution. Heading the first paragraph of each category would be a topic sentence that summarizes the discussion to follow. (The example of how to organize baseball equipment, discussed in Box 4.1, exemplifies a categorical design.)

CATEGORICAL-COMPARATIVE.   A categorical-comparative design compares two or more subjects for the purpose of enlightening each. This design works best for a comparative analysis, a message type popular in business and academia that features description, interpretation, and evaluation. A mistake writers commonly make when comparing two or more subjects is to discuss each one separately before moving on to the next. In effect, the subjects become the main headings, and the categories for comparison assume the role of subheadings. This type of structure makes it difficult to process subject comparisons because they are not made side-by-side, category-by-category. Box 5.1, for example, shows how *not* to organize a comparative analysis of three global businesses.

BOX 5.1

Company 1
Mission Statement
¶_____

Products and Services
¶_____

Company Sites
¶_____

Revenue and Income
¶_____

Employee Training and Development
¶_____

Company 2
Mission Statement
¶_____

Products and Services
¶_____

Company Sites
¶_____

Revenue and Income
¶_____

Employee Training and Development
¶_____

Company 3
Mission Statement
¶_____

Products and Services
¶_____

Company Sites
¶_____

Revenues and Income
¶_____

Employee Training and Development
¶_____

In this example (Box 5.1), readers are expected to remember how company 1 performed across five categories as they read about Company 2. Then, they must recall how Companies 1 and 2 compared as they learn about Company 3. Too much backtracking is asked of the reader.

A categorical-comparative design offers a better, more integrated way to organize these kinds of messages because readers immediately see how the subjects (the three companies) compare on each category, one category at a time (see Box 5.2).

BOX 5.2

Mission Statement
¶ (comparison of companies 1, 2, and 3)

Products and Services
¶ (comparison of companies 1, 2, and 3)

Company Sites
¶ (comparison of companies 1, 2, and 3)

Revenues and Income
¶ (comparison of companies 1, 2, and 3)

Employee Training and Development
¶ (comparison of companies 1, 2, and 3)

CAUSAL.   As noted in the discussion of causal propositions of fact, your message will follow a causal design when your overall purpose relies on establishing a causal relationship. Each of your main ideas may reflect a "stand-alone" causal relationship that directly supports your purpose. Or your main ideas may establish a causal relationship by building upon one another in support of your purpose. Here are examples of each approach:

Purpose statement: *Various events can cause an earthquake.*

   I. A ruptured geological fault can cause an earthquake.
  II. A volcanic eruption can cause an earthquake.
 III. A landslide can cause an earthquake.
  IV. A nuclear explosion can cause an earthquake.

Purpose statement: *The earthquake raised the cost of housing.*

   I. The earthquake destroyed many homes and apartments.
  II. Thousands of stranded homeowners and apartment dwellers needed new housing.
 III. The resulting shortage of available homes and apartments drove up prices.

Creating well-reasoned, well-evidenced causal arguments can preclude your readers from raising damaging counter-arguments to your position. Your analysis should account for these possibilities: Is there a direct causal relationship (cause = effect; effect = cause)? Or are there other, more likely causes of the effect than the cause(s) you offer? Do multiple causes, in addition to those you present, collectively produce the causal relationship? Does the cause(s) lead to other effects for which you have not accounted?

CHRONOLOGICAL/SEQUENTIAL.   A chronological design orders the elements of your message based on time. The chronology can start at any point in time and weave forth and back, but it will usually go from past to present or from present to past. When you give historical context to your subject and trace its temporal development, you are using a chronological design. If you were writing a paper on how the NCAA Basketball Tournament evolved into a 64-team contest, you could organize the body of your message along the lines of these topic sentences:

- The first NCAA Basketball Tournament, played in 1939, included eight teams.
- In 1951, twice as many teams, 16, were invited to the tournament.
- The tournament doubled to 32 teams in 1975.
- Within a six-year period, 1979–1985, the number of participating schools increased four more times, reaching its present number of 64 teams in 1985.
- Today, some have proposed increasing the tournament to 96 teams, with the top 32 teams having a first-round bye.

Similar to a chronological design, a sequential design is time based in the sense that it describes a step-by-step process or task. (The increasingly popular how-to message often uses a sequential design, where each step of the how-to process or task becomes a main idea.) If you were explaining how to report a car accident, your main ideas might read like this:

- First, determine if you, the other driver, any passengers, or any pedestrians are injured or may be injured.
- Call 911 to request medical help, if necessary, and to request police assistance.
- Once help is on its way, exchange insurance information with the other driver.
- Be sure to notify your insurance company within 24 hours of the accident.

NARRATIVE.   A narrative design allows you to present your message in the form of a story. Although a narrative design does not feature topic sentences or clearly labeled points, careful readers have little trouble picking out the story's main ideas. In a *New Yorker* article chronicling the lives of those who have committed suicide by jumping off San Francisco's Golden Gate Bridge, Tad Friend narrates:

On December 17, 2001, fourteen-year-old Marissa Imrie, a petite and attractive straight-A student who had planned to become a psychiatrist, left her second-period class at Santa Rosa High School, took a hundred-and-fifty-dollar taxi ride to the Golden Gate, and jumped to her death. Though Marissa was always very hard on herself and had lately complained of severe headaches and insomnia, her mother, Renee Milligan, had no inkling of her plans. "She called us 'the glue girls,' we were so close," Milligan told me. "She'd never spoken about the bridge, and we'd never even visited it."

When Milligan examined her daughter's computer afterward, she discovered that Marissa had been visiting a how-to Web site about suicide that featured grisly autopsy photos. The site notes that many suicide methods are ineffective (poison is fatal only fifteen per cent of the time, drug overdose twelve per cent, and wrist cutting a mere five per cent) and therefore recommends bridges, noting that "jumps from higher than . . . 250 feet over water are almost always fatal." Milligan bought the proprietor of the site's book, "Suicide and Attempted Suicide," and read the following sentence: "The Golden Gate Bridge is to suicides what Niagara Falls is to honeymooners." She returned the book and gave the computer away.

Every year, Marissa had written her mother a Christmas letter reflecting on the year's events. On Christmas Day that year, Milligan, going through her daughter's things, found her suicide note. It was tucked into "The Chronicles of Narnia," which sat beside a copy of "Seven Habits of Highly Effective Teenagers." The note ended with a plea: "Please forgive me. Don't shut yourselves off from the world. Everyone is better off without this fat, disgusting, boring girl. Move on."

Renee Milligan could not. "When I went to my optometrist, I realized he has big pictures of the Golden Gate in his office, and I had to walk out," she said. "The image of the bridge is everywhere. San Francisco is the Golden Gate Bridge—I can't escape it."*

Friend's narrative design functions every bit as powerfully as would a more direct, thesis-driven, topic sentence style to illustrate the lessons revealed by the tragedy of suicide. Young teenagers are not immune from depression. Spurred by negative, distorted perceptions of self-worth, they suffer alone, their pain unnoticed or unaddressed until it is too late. For the family they leave behind, the mourning never quite ends.

A message can combine different designs, leading to a variety of organizational possibilities. A categorical or categorical-comparative design can include a narrative that functions as a summary, a narrative can be told chronologically, a chronology can historically trace an evolving causal relationship, and so forth. Although these designs lend themselves to informative messages, they can be imported to persuasive messages as well. Whatever design you use to organize your message, however, it should facilitate the creation of a unified and coherent message.

REVISE HOW YOU REVISE: A FINAL NOTE

Throughout these pages, one of the recurring themes has been that the process of rewriting is enhanced when you create distance between you the writer and you the editor. Previous suggestions have included letting your writing

*Reprinted by permission of International Creative Management, Inc. Copyright © 2003 by Tad Friend.

"rest" between revisions so that its sense-making does not benefit from your being so close to the text; using a reverse outline to analyze your writing after-the-fact to reveal organizational problems you may not routinely detect; and seeing how a potential reader might organize and revise a sample of your writing.

Another way to create distance is to review and revise your message in different settings. Nearly all of us today type our first draft on a computer, where many of us also make all or most of our revisions. More experienced writers, though, usually alternate between editing onscreen and editing printed versions of their drafts. Both approaches have their advantages.

Onscreen revising allows you to quickly try out different versions of the same sentence or paragraph. When you revise your message, the onscreen image instantly reflects those changes. The resulting "clean" text, one free of handwritten revisions, is easier to read and assess, which facilitates even more instant revising. Onscreen word-processing programs also offer dictionaries, thesauruses, and tools for correcting spelling and grammar.

Revising a printed draft, on the other hand, elevates your critical perspective by distancing you more from the original digital draft. The mode of presentation (hard copy rather than digital) and the venue (somewhere away from your computer) alter your orientation, enabling you to approach the printed draft almost as if you were the reader, not the writer. The experience is similar to what happens when you read your writing aloud: You become more aware of what the text actually says.

A printed draft provides for a more nonlinear reading than does a digital draft. Although computers allow you to scroll down and jump from page to page, it is not the same as when your eyes scan a printed text. You interact with the text differently when it is scrolled rather than scanned. This is especially true when the printed text is physically spread on a table or posted on a wall. The ability to view multiple paragraphs and pages at once and to rapidly weave between paragraphs and pages without any of them digitally disappearing enables you to spot certain writing problems that do not come across as evidently on the computer screen. Organizational glitches will stand out, as will problems with topic sentences, unity and coherence, and language repetition.

RENO TIP **5.3**

RENOVATION TIP

If you work on the easier sections of your paper before tackling the harder parts, you are more likely to get into a creative rhythm that will boost your momentum and confidence. And you will be less disheartened if you take on the more challenging aspects of your paper *after*, rather than before, you have completed a substantial portion of your writing.

Chapter 5

EXERCISES

EXERCISE 1. Write an application letter for an ideal entry-level job position to which you aspire. Summarize your education, training, experience, and accomplishments using a verb-oriented style that minimally employs adjectives, adverbs, and the word *I*.

EXERCISE 2. In the following passage, which four sentences added from other sources disturb the unity of the paragraph? (from Oliver Wendell Holmes, Jr., "The Path of the Law," *Harvard Law Review* 10)

> When we study law we are not studying a mystery but a well-known profession. The law is reason free from passion. We are studying what we shall want in order to appear before judges, or to advise people in such a way as to keep them out of court. The reason why it is a profession, why people will pay lawyers to argue for them or to advise them, is that in societies like ours the command of the public force is intrusted to the judges in certain cases, and the whole power of the state will be put forth, if necessary, to carry out their judgments and decrees. Law without force is impotent. People want to know under what circumstances and how far they will run the risk of coming against what is so much stronger than themselves, and hence it becomes a business to find out when this danger is to be feared. It is dangerous to be right on matters on which the established authorities are wrong. The object of our study, then, is prediction, the prediction of the incidence of the public force through the instrumentality of the courts. In a government of laws, existence of the government will be imperiled if it fails to observe the law scrupulously.

EXERCISE 3. Arrange these sentences into a coherent paragraph that begins with this sentence: *To what extent can criminal trials be expected to establish the truth about historic events for journalists?* (from Edward Jay Epstein, *Between Fact and Fiction: The Problem of Journalism*)

A. In the popular imagination, however, a trial performs a somewhat grander service.

B. In law, the purpose of a criminal trial is to decide, according to predetermined rules, whether a defendant is guilty or not guilty of a particular charge.

C. The general assumption is that, if fairly conducted, a trial will yield the whole truth; aside from meting out justice to the accused, it will provide complete information and resolve the doubts of a concerned public.

D. Adversary proceedings are designed to render a simple yes-or-no answer to some precise question, a question which has been drawn in as specific a manner as possible.

E. The question is a serious one, but it has been confounded by a discrepancy that exists between the legal and journalistic expectation of what a trial does.

F. It is looked upon as a fact-finding operation, an occasion for the public exposure of all known information regarding a given crime.

EXERCISE 4. Arrange these sentences into a coherent paragraph that begins with this sentence: *Nobody ever discovered ugliness through photographs.* (from Susan Sontag, *On Photography*)

A. Even if someone did say that, all it would mean is: "I find that ugly thing . . . beautiful."

B. (The name under which Fox Talbot patented the photograph in 1841 was the calotype: from *kalos*, beautiful.)

C. But many, through photographs, have discovered beauty.

D. Nobody exclaims, "Isn't that ugly! I must take a photograph of it."

E. Except for those situations in which the camera is used to document, or to mark social rites, what moves people to take photographs is finding something beautiful.

EXERCISE 5. Arrange these sentences into a coherent paragraph. (from Edwin Black, *Rhetorical Criticism: A Study in Method*)

A. Having, as it sometimes seems, the key to the universe in its very techniques of investigation, science is on a progress of discovery that has no conceivable limit, unless it is the mushroom cloud on the horizon.

B. It is no wonder that we respect the office of scientist, for one mystery after another has yielded to the formidable machinery of scientific method.

C. He is consulted by senators, courted by corporations, and exalted by the popular mind.

D. The scientist is one of the cultural heroes of our age.

E. The triumphs of science seem inexorable as the tide.

F. And with the mysteries, so also numberless human afflictions are closer to our control: hunger and squalor, pain and neurotic anguish, enervating toil and terrifying superstition, perhaps, as Bergson once dared hope, even death itself.

PART II

Additional Tools

6 Punctuation Unmasked

WHY, IS PUNCTUATION; SO/IMPORTANT.

Punctuation helps to structure and explain your sentences, allowing your audience to understand more easily what you mean. Primarily, it lets your reader know when to pause and when to stop, how elements in the sentence relate and connect, and which elements occupy superior versus subordinate status. Proper punctuation especially aids in the readability of long sentences.

In an often-cited example of how punctuation conveys meaning, a college professor asked his students how they would punctuate this sentence: *Woman without her man is nothing.* Depending on the student's perspective, one of two choices emerged: *Woman without her man is nothing. Woman: without her, man is nothing.*

The effective use of punctuation leads to powerful sentences that, beyond being correct and understandable, drive home your message. A well-placed colon, for example, enables you to make your point quickly and strikingly. Nowhere is this better illustrated than in Ernest Hemingway's famous proposal for a six-word short story: *For sale: Baby shoes, never worn.*

Knowing how to use punctuation also augments your credibility. It reflects your literacy and assists you in writing sentences that, in turn, elevate your perceived competence. Too, because so many people have so much trouble with even the simplest of marks, a proficiency in punctuation distinguishes you from the crowd, increasing your worth to nearly any organization or employer.

If you have had trouble with punctuation in the past, it is probably not because of the subject's difficulty or your inability to grasp the material. Rather, most people who struggle with punctuation either have never paid much attention to the rules or had them explained in ways that were daunting.

English punctuation comprises these 14 marks that can be broadly categorized by their functions, which sometimes overlap:

- Periods, question marks, and exclamation points let the reader know when a sentence has ended and whether it is declaring, asking, or exclaiming.
- Commas, semicolons, and colons separate, connect, or introduce ideas.
- Apostrophes usually reveal possession, or who "owns" certain elements in the sentence.
- Double and single quotation marks indicate the words of another speaker or writer.
- Ellipses and slashes save space while signaling that something has been left out of the sentence.
- Dashes, parentheses, and brackets provide ways to emphasize or subordinate ideas or provide additional information.

Note: The guidelines that follow are appropriate for most writing, but the style manuals of particular disciplines may vary slightly.

PERIODS, QUESTION MARKS, AND EXCLAMATION POINTS

Periods

The most common use of a period is to end a sentence. Like the question mark and the exclamation point, it tells the reader to stop.

- This is an example of a sentence that ends with a period.
- Most sentences end with periods.
- If a sentence does not end with a period, it will likely end with a question mark or an exclamation point.

When a sentence ends with a (double) quotation mark, the period goes inside, or before, the quotation mark. Even if just one word has been quoted, the period goes inside. This is standard American English; the British place periods (and commas) outside, or after, a final (single) quotation mark.

When a sentence ends with a parenthetical comment, the period follows the closing parenthesis. If the parenthetical material stands alone as a complete sentence, the period goes before the closing parenthesis. When a parenthetical sentence is part of another sentence (this parenthetical sentence is an example), it is not capitalized or punctuated at the end. And, as seen in the last sentence, a comma can come after a closing parenthesis, but it cannot come before an opening parenthesis. If the parenthetical information, such as a citation source, comes after a sentence ending in a quotation mark, most style manuals recommend placing the period after the parenthesis. For example, "The most common use of a period is to end a sentence" (Kallan 100).

Periods come after abbreviations (misc., Mr., Ms., fax no., etc.) and when numbers or letters are used to identify items in a vertical list.

1. [first item]   A. [first item]
2. [second item]   B. [second item]
3. [third item]   C. [third item]

Periods are not needed when parentheses enclose numbers and letters: (1), (2), (3); (A), (B), (C).

Periods can be used to provide visual closure at the end of phrases and single words. In resumes, the writer may use a period to indicate the end of one entry and the start of another.

Question Marks

When a sentence poses a direct question, it ends with a question mark.

- When is it appropriate to end a sentence with a question mark? Can you give me an example?
- Didn't you just give me two?
- Did I?

If you have a series of questions continuing from another question or a declarative sentence, punctuate them with question marks even if they are not complete sentences. *Where did you learn how to use a question mark so effectively? In junior high? High school? College? Or was it when you dated that Philosophy major?*

Do not use a question mark when posing an indirect question. An indirect question paraphrases your own or someone else's question in a way that it is no longer a direct inquiry. *I wonder whether I am using too many question marks or not using enough. My professors have asked why I care so much about question marks and why I don't just focus on writing clearly, concisely, and compellingly.*

When your sentence concludes with quoted material ending in a question, the mark goes inside the closing quotation mark. *I just finished reading a great article, "Should Punctuation Be Taught in Kindergarten?"* The question mark is part of the article's title and must be included within the quoted title. If the title does not end with a question mark, but you, the writer, raise the question, the mark goes outside the title. *Have you read "Punctuation Must Be Taught in Kindergarten"?* If your quoted material ends with a question mark and you are asking a question of your reader, one question mark suffices. *Have you read "Should Punctuation Be Taught in Kindergarten?"* If you want to exclaim about quoted material that ends with a question mark, that mark takes precedence over an exclamation point. *Stop, drop everything, and immediately read "Should Punctuation Be Taught in the Kindergarten?"*

Exclamation Points

An exclamation point normally comes at the end of the sentence.

- I love exclamation points! They're great! They're amazing! They're marvelous!
- Stop it! You're using too many exclamation points!
- Don't tell me what to do!

Exclamation points should be used sparingly. Their overuse suggests a young, somewhat out-of-control writer who does not yet possess sufficient skills to express intensity linguistically.

The positioning of the exclamation point with quoted material follows the same logic guiding the question mark. When your sentence concludes with quoted material ending in an exclamation point, it goes inside the closing quotation mark. *I just finished reading a great article, "Punctuation Must Be Taught in Kindergarten!"* (The exclamation point is part of the title.) When you, the writer, exclaim, the exclamation point goes outside the quotation. *Everyone should read "Punctuation Must Be Taught in Kindergarten"!* If your quoted material ends with an exclamation point and you want to exclaim as well, a single exclamation point suffices. *I love "Punctuation Must Be Taught in Kindergarten!"* If you were to pose a question about the article, the article's exclamation point would still end the sentence. *Have you ever read "Punctuation Must Be Taught in Kindergarten!"*

COMMAS, SEMICOLONS, AND COLONS

Commas

The comma is the most difficult form of punctuation to master because it serves several purposes; the rules governing its use can be difficult to apply, even when you know the rules; and some sentences require an added comma to avoid confusion, despite there being no formal rule for its addition. The comma plays a key role in aiding readability and minimizing confusion.

    1. A comma and a coordinating conjunction can join two independent clauses. An independent clause contains a subject and a predicate and can stand alone as a sentence; a dependent clause contains a subject and a predicate but cannot stand alone as a sentence, usually because it begins with a subordinating word. The seven coordinating conjunctions are *and, but, for, or, nor, so,* and *yet.* (One way of remembering them is by the acronym FANBOYS.)

    Consider these two sentences: *I like what William Safire says about writing. I love what H. W. Fowler says about writing.* Although the sentences are punctuated correctly (a period can always follow a stand-alone independent clause), they do not effectively convey the larger thought addressed by both sentences: the distinction between whom you like versus whom you love. Expressing this thought in two sentences distances its related parts by separating them. A better approach would be to join the two independent clauses. You could do this by using a comma and a coordinating conjunction. *I like what William Safire says about writing, and I love what H. W. Fowler says about writing.* Or: *I like what William Safire says about writing, but I love what H. W. Fowler says about writing.* When you have two independent clauses that are short and well balanced, you do not need a comma before the coordinating conjunction when, without the comma, the sentence is still easy to read. *I like William Safire but I love H. W. Fowler.*

    2. Commas separate three or more items in a series.

- Darla understood how to structure a sentence, support an argument, and use punctuation correctly.
- Darla helped Sue, Beverly, and Wilbur with their writing.

A comma is not used when a series contains only two items. You would *not* write *Darla helped Sue, and Beverly with their writing.* Some guides, such as the *Associated Press Stylebook and Briefing on Media Law 2011* (AP Stylebook), which is used mainly by newspapers, leave out the comma before the *and* in a series. Other manuals suggest it is optional. The more popular advice today is to add the comma to avoid the sort of potential confusion seen in these examples:

- "Among those interviewed were his two ex-wives, Kris Kristofferson and Robert Duval." (from a *Los Angeles Times* story about Merle Haggard)
- He liked fast cars, barbequed steaks and cats.

Had a comma been added before the "and" in each sentence, it would have been clearer that Kris Kristofferson and Robert Duval are not ex-wives and that cats are not being barbequed along with steaks.

3. Commas set off nonrestrictive elements. Restrictive and nonrestrictive elements usually take the form of adjectival and adverbial clauses, adjectival phrases, and appositives. A nonrestrictive or nonessential element is one that does not significantly affect the meaning of the sentence. When you set off a nonrestrictive element with commas, you are saying that it can be omitted without major consequence. A restrictive or essential element, on the other hand, determines or restricts the meaning of what it modifies. Because a restrictive modifier alters the point of the sentence, it cannot be set off by commas.

Restrictive and nonrestrictive elements appear frequently as adjectival clauses and phrases. Adjectival clauses and phrases function as adjectives. They modify nouns or pronouns by answering the questions, *which one* (Which student got an A in the course?), *what kind* (What kind of student usually gets an A in the course?), and *how many* (How many students usually get an A in the course?). Adjectival clauses and phrases usually begin with words such as *that, which, who,* and *whom.* Compare these sentences:

- The professor who best exemplifies a commitment to students will win the Professor of the Year award.
- The professor, whom I once met, won the Professor of the Year award.

In the first sentence, the modifying clause (*who best exemplifies a commitment to students*) is central to the purpose of the sentence because it tells the reader who will win the award. In the second sentence, the modifying clause (*whom I once met*) is nonrestrictive because it does not affect the point of the sentence, which is true regardless of whether I had ever met the professor.

When *that* and *which* are used, *that* introduces a restrictive modifier and *which* usually introduces a nonrestrictive modifier. (Some accomplished writers, however, continue to use *which* with restrictive modifiers.) Examples of the traditional approach:

- The speech that the mayor gave was hailed as the most eloquent of the day's presentations.
- The mayor's speech, which ran ten minutes, was hailed as the most eloquent of the day's presentations, which lasted about two hours.

Sometimes only personal knowledge can determine whether the modifying language, such as an appositive, should be restrictive or nonrestrictive. (An appositive phrase renames, or defines, the noun or pronoun that immediately precedes it.) Both of the following sentences, for example, could be correct:

- Glenn showered his wife Jane with expensive gifts.
- Glenn showered his wife, Jane, with expensive gifts.

The first sentence is correct if Glenn is married to more than one woman; the sentence must reference a specific wife by name for the audience to know which wife received the expensive gifts. The wife's name, *Jane*, is restrictive and appears in the text without commas. The second sentence is correct if Glenn has one wife. Eliminating *Jane* from the sentence does not affect its meaning because *wife* cannot refer to anyone other than Jane.

And should Glenn and Jane have one daughter, it would be correct to say that *Glenn and Jane's daughter, Victoria, loves talking about restrictive and nonrestrictive modifiers*. But if Glenn and Jane have more than one daughter, *Victoria* becomes restrictive and the sentence must read, *Glenn and Jane's daughter Victoria loves talking about restrictive and nonrestrictive modifiers*.

The difference between restrictive and nonrestrictive explains why seemingly similar sentences are punctuated differently.

- Harper Lee's bestselling novel, *To Kill a Mockingbird*, should be required reading for every high school student.
- John Steinbeck's bestselling novel *The Grapes of Wrath* should be required reading for every high school student.

Because Lee wrote only one bestselling novel, *bestselling novel* cannot refer to anything other than *To Kill a Mockingbird*. Steinbeck, in contrast, wrote several bestsellers. If *The Grapes of Wrath* were omitted from the sentence, the reader would have no idea which Steinbeck novel the writer had in mind. Both sentences are punctuated correctly.

4. Commas separate introductory clauses and phrases from the rest of sentence. Most often, they are adverbial clauses or phrases, transitional phrases or words, participial phrases, or absolute phrases.

Adverbial clauses and phrases function as adverbs. They modify verbs, adjectives, other adverbs, and even entire sentences. Modifying a verb, they may tell when, where, how, how often, to what degree, or why the action occurred in the sentence. Adverbial clauses and phrases begin with words such as *after, although, because, before, even though, if, when, unless, until*, and *while*.

- Although she never completed a creative writing class, she became an award-winning novelist.
- After he took his eleventh creative writing course, he decided he was ready to start his first short story.
- When she saw him at conferences, she always asked how his writing was progressing.
- If he had not been her womanizing ex-husband, she would have tried to help him with his writing.

When an adverbial clause or phrase comes in the middle of a sentence, immediately after the subject and before the predicate, it is set off by commas. *His first short story, although only 55 words long, took him three months to write.* When an adverbial clause comes at the end of the sentence and is essential or restrictive, no comma precedes it. *He attended writing conferences because they inspired him to write.* A nonessential or nonrestrictive adverbial clause coming at the end of a sentence, however, is set off by a comma. *Critics called her a great novelist, although she said she was still learning how to write.*

You may choose to omit a comma after a short introductory adverbial clause or phrase. *When I study I rarely fail any classes. By Friday I will know my grade.*

Transitional phrases and words help the reader by labeling and bridging the writer's thoughts. Frequently, writers will say *first, for example, in addition, in conclusion, in fact, in other words, last,* and *of course.* Many transitional words are conjunctive adverbs, such as *consequently, finally, furthermore, hence, however, indeed, moreover, otherwise, then, thus, subsequently,* and *therefore.* When transitional phrases and words come at the beginning or end of a sentence, they are set off by a comma; when they come in the middle of a sentence, they are preceded and followed by commas. *Finally, any discussion of commas, moreover, is complicated but still worth the effort, however.*

Participial phrases, which modify nouns and pronouns in much the same way as an adjective would, feature a verb form ending in *-ing* (present participle) or in *-ed* or the past tense equivalent (past participle) that does not function as a verb within the participial phrase.

- Recognizing he wrote slowly, he decided he needed to spend more than 15 minutes a day working on his term paper.
- Recognized as a slow writer by nearly everyone, he decided he needed to spend more than 15 minutes a day working on his term paper.

If the introductory clause or phrase becomes the subject of the sentence and is followed by a verb rather than a subject, no comma follows the clause or phrase. *Recognizing that he wrote slowly motivated him to spend more than 15 minutes a day working on his term paper.*

Absolute phrases feature a noun or pronoun followed by a participle. They modify the entire sentence. *Her knowledge of punctuation now improving, she decided she would invite the handsome English major to dinner.* Or: *She decided she would invite the handsome English major to dinner, her knowledge of punctuation having improved.*

5. Commas separate coordinating adjectives. Two or more adjectives are coordinate if you can change their order, or join them by *and*, and the sentence still makes sense. Take this example: *She lives in an orange, two-story, older house.* If you reverse the order of the adjectives—*She lives in an older, orange, two-story house*—their function and the meaning they convey remain unchanged; each adjective still modifies the noun *house.*

Adjectives are noncoordinating or cumulative when they do not directly modify a noun or pronoun. Cumulative adjectives are not separated by commas because they essentially represent one set of adjectives. *The Teachers Museum includes several designer leather briefcases.* In this sentence, *leather* modifies *briefcases, designer* modifies *leather briefcases,* and *several* modifies *designer leather briefcases.* Unlike coordinating adjectives, the order of cumulative adjectives cannot be reversed and still make sense. *The Teachers Museum includes leather, designer, several briefcases.*

6. Commas set off parenthetical material that appears in the middle or at the end of a sentence. Using commas, as opposed to parentheses or dashes, interrupts the reading experience less because the parenthetical material is integrated into the grammatical structure of the sentence; thus, the material is also emphasized less.

- Parenthetical comments, it should be remembered, are not essential to understanding the point of the sentence.
- My lifelong study of parenthetical comments has been worth it, or maybe not.

7. Commas set off contrasting elements that appear in the beginning, middle, or end of the sentence.

- Darlene, not George, excelled at punctuating contrasting elements.
- Darlene excelled at punctuating contrasting elements, not George.
- Unlike George, Darlene excelled at punctuating contrasting elements.

8. Commas set off the source of an indirect quotation (or paraphrase) when attribution is given within the sentence.

- Teaching her students how to correctly punctuate indirect quotations, Professor Dawn declared, would be her life's calling.
- The success of her mission, however, might take a while, she had to continually tell herself.

9. Commas separate the elements in a date. They set off the year from the month and day, as well as from the rest of the sentence. Commas are not needed when the day precedes the month, a day does not follow the month, or a holiday comes in place of the month.

- We met on June 20, 2011, at the International Conference on Commas.
- We met on 20 June 2011 at the International Conference on Commas.
- We met in June 2011 at the International Conference on Commas.
- We met on Labor Day 2011 to discuss the upcoming International Conference on Commas.

10. Commas set off the elements of an address. Separate street, city, and state by commas; do not separate the zip code by a comma unless more information follows the zip code.

- 3801 West Temple Avenue, Pomona, CA 91768
- Send your comments and suggestions to Richard Kallan, Chair, Department of Communication, 3801 West Temple Avenue, Pomona, CA 91768, in an envelope, however large it may need to be.

11. Commas serve additional purposes, including the setting off of *yes/no* responses, tag questions, and words and phrases of direct address.

- Yes, I will mentor the tennis team on the ins and outs of proper punctuation.
- I think that not charging the tennis players for my mentoring is a good idea, don't you?
- Coach, call me and let know what you think of my idea. My fellow Americans, please do the same.

Commas are also used in place of omitted words and after popular, informal abbreviations, such as *i.e.* (from the Latin *id est*, meaning *that is*), *e.g.* (from the Latin *exempli gratia*, meaning *for example*), and etc. (the abbreviation for *et cetera*, meaning *and so forth*). In formal writing, *i.e.* and *e.g.* are placed in parentheses along with the text that follows, and *etc.* is spelled out.

- In the end, many tennis players struggled with the intricacies and nuances of commas; others, with semicolons and colons; and some, with dashes and parentheses.
- I also helped (i.e., somewhat improved) the punctuation skills of several football players, especially some on the offensive team (e.g., the quarterback and the center), by giving them rules, tips, advice, et cetera for using punctuation effectively.

12. A comma is sometimes needed to avoid confusion or misinterpretation.

ORIGINAL	The lion was finally able to run after the veterinarian performed hip replacement surgery.
REVISION	The lion was finally able to run, after the veterinarian performed hip replacement surgery.
ORIGINAL	Those who can teach; those who cannot criticize.
REVISION	Those who can, teach; those who cannot, criticize.
ORIGINAL	It was Bob Dylan saw reading *Renovating Your Writing*.
REVISION	It was Bob, Dylan saw reading *Renovating Your Writing*.

Semicolons

Use a semicolon, which provides more pause than a comma does but less than a period does, to unite closely related independent clauses.

It has been shown how a comma and a coordinating conjunction can join two independent clauses. *I like what William Safire says about writing, but I love what H. W. Fowler says about writing.* Another approach would be to replace the comma and coordinating conjunction with a semicolon. *I like Safire; I love Fowler.* The semicolon here, compared to using a comma and a coordinating conjunction, affords an even closer pairing of the two clauses, creating a stronger and somewhat more elegant statement. The semicolon alone will not establish this close relationship; it only provides the tool for conveying it. (The previous sentence demonstrates how a semicolon links related independent clauses that cannot easily be joined by a comma and a coordinating conjunction.)

A semicolon can also join two independent clauses when the second begins with a conjunctive adverb. Writers often try to connect such clauses by placing a comma before the conjunctive adverb, thinking the adverb serves as a coordinating conjunction. This results in a type of run-on sentence called a *comma splice. I am not a good writer, however, I know how to use semicolons.* The sentence can be correctly revised in several ways:

- I am not a good writer; however, I know how to use semicolons.
- I am not a good writer; I know how to use semicolons, however.
- I am not a good writer, but I know how to use semicolons.
- I am not a good writer. However, I know how to use semicolons.
- Although I know how to use semicolons, I am not a good writer.

In the first example, the sentence would be punctuated the same if you were to replace *however* with *consequently, hence, moreover, subsequently,* or *therefore.* Whenever you have a conjunctive adverb that begins the second of two joined independent clauses, delete any comma preceding the conjunctive adverb and replace it with a semicolon; then add a comma after the conjunctive adverb.

Like conjunctive adverbs, transitional phrases and words cannot join two independent clauses unless preceded by a semicolon, not a comma.

Original	I know how to use semicolons, in fact it's my favorite thing to do.
Revision	I know how to use semicolons; in fact, it's my favorite thing to do.

You can use a semicolon before a coordinating conjunction if either independent clause has internal punctuation (CMS takes mild exception, recommending a semicolon only when the second independent clause includes internal punctuation); or the clauses, although paired, communicate antithesis; or the clauses mandate more separation because of their complicated and potentially confusing structure. A comma, instead of a semicolon, before the coordinating conjunction would suffice in the examples that follow, but the semicolon makes the sentence a little easier to read by providing greater pause between the independent clauses.

- In college, where he honed his writing skills, he learned the rules of punctuation, so they could help him express ideas more clearly, concisely, and compellingly; and he embarked on a lasting relationship with grammar that would prove just as beneficial in his quest to become a famous author.
- They were taught every form of punctuation again and again from the time they entered high school until they graduated college; but they mastered none until they went to prison.
- Although she refuses to show any of her graded papers to the staff at the Tutorial Center, she says she does poorly on writing assignments, and thus needs everyone's help, because she has difficulty concentrating or even remembering the requirements of the assignment; or is she just claiming to perform poorly so she can get additional free tutoring?

Use commas in a simple series (*I like dogs, cats, birds, horses, and rabbits.*), but when an item includes internal punctuation, use semicolons to set off the items so the reader can tell where one ends and another begins. *I like dogs, especially those belonging to the sporting, nonsporting, and working groups and if the dogs like rabbits; cats, if they are well behaved, which they usually are, except for the last one I adopted; birds; horses, but only if they are Arabians, Appaloosas, or Clydesdales, and they get along with dogs, cats, and birds; and rabbits.* When the items in a series are long and complex, use semicolons to aid readability. *He liked dogs because they were affectionate, loyal, and protective, and he felt safe in their presence; cats because they were independent and saved him a lot of money by ridding his seven homes of mice and other rodents; and horses because he lived in the country and could always count on them as an alternative form of transportation.*

Colons

Use a colon after an independent clause when what follows defines, elaborates upon, or summarizes elements in the clause.

- She got A's on the two tests that mattered most: the midterm and the final.
- Knowing how to use punctuation will change your life: You will get better grades, better jobs, and smarter dates.
- They know nothing about grammar, punctuation, usage, or mechanics: Clearly, they are not the best writers in the class.

A sentence structured with a colon flags the attention of the reader because it promises more to come, but not before a staged pause (the colon) and a metaphorical drum roll. Colons can effectively frame bold statements and pointed questions.

- Asked whether I could ever be friends with someone who did not care about semicolons and colons, my answer was unequivocal: I could not.
- The student never came to class and failed all three exams on grammar and punctuation, leading the professor to wonder: Why is this student a writing tutor?

Whether you capitalize the first word (other than a proper noun) of an independent clause that follows a colon depends on the style manual you follow. MLA, APA, and CMS have different guidelines on this matter, although it is common to capitalize the first word of a question introduced by a colon. Should a colon introduce more than one sentence, all are capitalized.

A colon follows an independent clause that introduces a list. *I particularly like these forms of punctuation: commas, semicolons, and colons.* Do not break an otherwise fluid sentence by placing a colon after a verb or preposition (or a phrase like *such as*) that immediately precedes a list. In these examples, no colon is needed:

- My favorite punctuation marks *are* commas, semicolons, and colons.
- My favorite punctuation marks *include* . . .
- My favorite punctuation marks *include, for example,* . . .
- I have a good knowledge *of* . . .
- I use many forms of punctuation, *such as* . . .

A colon follows a formal salutation (*Dear Professor Kallan:*). In informal salutations, a comma suffices (*Dear Rich,*).

A colon separates a title from its subtitle (*Renovating Your Writing: Shaping Ideas into Clear, Concise, and Compelling Messages*).

A colon follows an incomplete sentence that informally introduces a thought coming on the heels of another. Recall, for instance, how *Or* was used a few pages back in introducing the second of two examples: "*I like what William Safire says about writing, and I love what H. W. Fowler says about writing. Or: I like what William Safire says about writing, but I love what H. W. Fowler says about writing.*"

Use colons when expressing the time of day (6:30 PM); the minutes, hours, and seconds of a time period (2:31:16); ratios (4:1); Biblical references to chapter and verse (Psalm 23:4); memorandum headings (To: / From: / Date: / Subject:); and source citations that include the publisher's name and location (Boston: Pearson).

APOSTROPHES

The main purpose of an apostrophe is to indicate possession. Add an apostrophe and an *-s* (*'s*) after the last letter of the word to form the possessive of a singular noun.

SINGULAR	SINGULAR POSSESSIVE
boy	boy's dog . . .
girl	girl's
child	child's
man	man's
woman	woman's

Place an apostrophe after the *-s* (*s'*) to form the possessive of a plural noun ending in *-s* or *-es*. Add *'s* for plural nouns not ending in *-s* or *-es*.

PLURAL	PLURAL POSSESSIVE
boys	boys' dog . . .
girls	girls'
Joneses	Joneses'
children	children's
men	men's
women	women's

Singular nouns ending in *-s* are normally made possessive by adding *'s*: for example, *press's responsibility, Leon Uris's novel, Marion Jones's Olympic medals*. Most style manuals follow this rule, with the notable exception of the AP Stylebook, which requires adding only an apostrophe to form the possessive of any word ending in *-s* (*the press' responsibility, Leon Uris' novel, Marion Jones' Olympic medals*).

The conventional approach when forming the plural of "challenging" singular nouns ending in *-s* is to let the sound of the construction govern your decision-making and to avoid adding *'s* if it hampers pronunciation. Words ending in *-s* and having an *-s* in the middle, for example, create a phonetic obstacle when *'s* is added. Try saying Jesus's, Moses's, and Demosthenes's. In its most recent edition, however, CMS advises against using only an apostrophe to signify the possessive of these and similar words. Reversing an earlier position, CMS "no longer recommends the traditional exception for proper classical names of two or more syllables that end in an *eez* sound." Whereas *Euripides' tragedies* was once correct, now it is *Euripides's tragedies*. On the other hand, CMS recommends using an apostrophe after the *-s* when both the singular and plural forms of the noun end in *-s*, as in *politics, economics,* and *species*. In such cases, an apostrophe after the *s* forms the singular and plural possessive. Similarly, *United States'* is the correct possessive form.

When two nouns share ownership, the *'s* goes on the second noun. *Norman and Carmen's library contained hundreds of books on punctuation.* Or: *The library containing hundred of books on punctuation was Norman and Carmen's.* If Norman and Carmen individually own libraries, both nouns would be possessive: *Norman's and Carmen's libraries . . .* Or: *The libraries . . . are Norman's and Carmen's.*

To make compound nouns (singular nouns formed by two or more words) possessive, add *'s* to the last element in the noun: for example, *sister-in-law's, secretary of state's, attorney general's, chief executive officer's,* and *associate vice president's.*

Possessive pronouns, such as *his, hers, its, ours, theirs, yours,* and *whose*, do not take apostrophes. This rule must be followed, no *ands, ifs, buts,* or *maybes*.

Apostrophes take the place of the left out letters in contractions, such as *I'm, can't, we'll, we're,* and *should've*. In more colloquial venues, apostrophes substitute for letters and numbers. *Nothin' happenin' 'cause I'm just hangin' and chillin' and trying to sound like I wasn't really born in '68, or was it '69?*

An *'s* is used to form a plural when adding *s* alone might be confusing. *She used to get B's in all her classes until she became a punctuation guru. Now she gets A's, except for the two I's she received when she dropped out of school briefly to attend Punctuation Rehab.* The apostrophe here prevents the reader from confusing A's, B's, and I's with As, Bs, and Is. (MLA recommends adding *'s* when pluralizing any capital letter, but other style guides disagree with this practice.) For the sake of clarity, most guides call for using an apostrophe when pluralizing all lower case letters (*a's, b's, c's,* instead of *as, bs, cs*).

The trend is away from using *'s* to form plurals of letter abbreviations and more toward adding just *-s*: for example, *BAs, PhDs, CDs, PCs, CPUs, URLs*. The plurals of dates and numbers follow suit; today it is more common to see *1990s, six 5s,* and *four threes*.

DOUBLE AND SINGLE QUOTATION MARKS

Use quotation marks to indicate that you are quoting the words of others. *Famed sports writer Red Smith said: "There's nothing to writing. All you do is sit down at a typewriter and open a vein."* The source, *Red Smith*, can also appear after, as well as in the middle, of the quotation.

- "There's nothing to writing. All you do is sit down at a typewriter and open a vein," said Red Smith.
- "There's nothing to writing," Red Smith said. "All you do is sit down at a typewriter and open a vein."

- "There's nothing to writing. All you do is sit down at a typewriter," said Red Smith, "and open a vein."

When you interject the source within the quotation, the quotation marks must stop and start before and after each interjection.

Periods (unless parenthetical material follows the quotation) and commas always go inside, or before, the ending quotation mark. Semicolons and colons, however, go outside, or after the mark.

When you informally introduce a quotation with *Smith said* or some variation (for example, *Smith asked, Smith confessed, Smith declared, Smith exclaimed, Smith noted, Smith observed, Smith proclaimed, Smith stated,* and *Smith wrote*), a comma follows the introduction. A sentence that formally introduces a quotation ends with a colon. *Smith described the writing process in this way:* Whether formal or informal, an introduction to a quotation of two sentences or longer ends with a colon.

When introducing a quotation, you may change the first word to upper or lower case to fit the context of your sentence. If your therapist tells you to relax and says, "Fortunately, most punctuation marks are easy to learn," you could write:

- My therapist says that "fortunately, most punctuation marks are easy to learn."
- My therapist says, "Most punctuation marks are easy to learn."

Only where textual precision is mandated must you indicate changes in capitalization by bracketing the first letter of the word you changed. Had the preceding examples qualified, they would have taken this form:

- My therapist says that "[f]ortunately, most punctuation marks are easy to learn."
- My therapist says, "[M]ost punctuation marks are easy to learn."

When you introduce a quotation by integrating it with your own words to form a seamless construction, punctuate the sentence just as you would normally.

- My therapist believes that "most punctuation marks are easy to learn."
- My therapist preaches three things: writers are made not born, grammar is enjoyable, and "most punctuation marks are easy to learn."
- My therapist said that once upon a time, "most punctuation marks were easy to learn."

Use single quotation marks when your quoted material includes the following: quotations from other sources; text typically placed in quotation marks, such as the titles of articles, short stories, poems, book chapters, and other works; or specific words called out by quotation marks (discussed more at the end of this section).

- Don Watson, author of *Death Sentences*, writes: "Martin Amis might be right. 'The professionalism of ordinary existence: this is the enemy within.' Language, after all, defines ordinary existence. 'Speak, that I may see thee.' It's how we know each other."

- In *Expletive Deleted*, Ruth Wajnryb says: "There are two potential points of confusion when it comes to understanding and talking about foul language. One has to do with the words used that commonly *constitute* 'swearing.' The other has to do with how we *refer* to 'swearing.'"
- Constance Hale observes in *Sin and Syntax*: "Editors also use the royal *we* (calling it 'the editorial we'). Remember all those 'Talk of the Town' pieces in pre-Tina *New Yorker*? Lesser mortals—and writers not yet in *New Yorker* nirvana—might want to heed Mark Twain's advice, 'Only presidents, editors, and people with tapeworms ought to have the right to use *we*.'"

Longer quotations should be separated from the body of your text and formatted as an indented block of type without quotation marks. (In a block quotation, use double quotation marks to indicate when the quotation includes quotations from other sources or material normally placed in quotation marks.) Style manuals differ about when the length of quoted material requires blocking. MLA says to set off quotations of five lines or more, APA requires they be 40 words or longer, and CMS opts for 100 words or more ("at least six to eight lines of text") or when the quotation is two or more paragraphs long. Because they generally run more than two sentences, block quotations are usually introduced with a colon, although they can be introduced with a period-ending sentence if the sentence and the block quotation form a fluid narrative. A text having a blocked quotation would look something like this:

> In *Simple and Direct: A Rhetoric for Writers*, Jacques Barzun writes:
>
> A good judge of the facts has declared: "All writing is rewriting." He meant good writing, for easy reading. The path to rewriting is obvious: when rereading after a shorter or longer lapse of time what one has written, one feels dissatisfaction with this or that word, sentence, paragraph—or possibly with the whole effort, the essay or chapter. . . . If words you have set down puzzle you once you have forgotten how they came to your mind, they will puzzle the stranger and you must do something about them. . . .

In block quotations of one paragraph or less, the first line is not indented; quotations of two or more paragraphs should match the paragraphing of the original text.

When you paraphrase someone else's writing, you must characterize it entirely in your own words; it is not sufficient to change a few lines here and there. You must also cite the source that inspired your paraphrase. Quotation marks will be needed to identify only those words of your paraphrase, if any, that remain identical to the original. This is how you might paraphrase the Barzun quotation:

> In *Simple and Direct: A Rhetoric for Writers*, Jacques Barzun contends that writing is essentially the act of rewriting. To create a well-written piece that is easy to read, Barzun maintains, you have to let your writing set for a while. After you pick it up again, you will sense "dissatisfaction with this or that word, sentence, paragraph" and know it needs to be changed. When you are unsure what your writing means because you cannot recall what you originally intended to say, imagine how it will "puzzle the stranger" reading your words for the first time.

When quoting dialogue, begin a new paragraph every time the dialogue shifts to a new speaker, regardless of whether the speaker's name accompanies the quoted words. This allows the reader to follow along more easily.

"I dreamt of someday having an argument with you about punctuation *and winning.*"

"That's happened. You've won sometimes."

"No, I haven't."

"Yes, you have."

"No."

"Yes."

"No. You're too good. Always so logical, so prepared, so focused."

"Ok, maybe I am. Maybe . . . "

"Just say it."

"Ok, you've never won an argument with me!"

"Until now."

When a speaker's words extend to several paragraphs, place quotation marks at the start of each new paragraph, but assign a closing quotation mark only after the last word of the final quoted paragraph.

Quotation marks can be employed in lieu of italics to call attention to specific words referenced or defined within a sentence. *People use the word "grammar" to refer to a slew of writing problems, some of which deal with "usage," or the way in which language is customarily used.* Writers sometimes place quotation marks around selected words as a way of editorializing, usually negatively. *Some "experts" downplay the importance of punctuation and insist that beginning writers need to learn "more important" things.* Quotation marks in this context are meant to suggest the same disdain one conveys by using air quotes. These mocking tactics can be interpreted as snide and should be used cautiously.

ELLIPSES AND SLASHES

Ellipses

The main purpose of an ellipsis (plural, *ellipses*) is to indicate the omission of one or more words from a quotation. When the omission occurs in the middle of a quoted sentence, you insert an ellipsis where the text would ordinarily have gone. An ellipsis is three dots (represented by period marks . . .) with a space before and after each dot. When you omit the end of a quoted sentence, the ellipsis follows a sentence-ending period. This period comes before the ellipsis and is punctuated as you would a normal period, which this sentence will now illustrate. . . . (CMS takes a different view, advising that an ellipsis is not needed "after the last word of a quotation, even if the end of the original sentence has been omitted, unless the sentence as quoted is deliberately incomplete.") If, however, you omit the end of a sentence that ends in a question mark or an exclamation point, the mark or point comes after your ellipsis if the truncated sentence still raises a question or expresses exclamation. *"Aren't all these distinctions fun . . . ?"* Generally, punctuation in the original quotation that immediately precedes or follows your insertion of an ellipsis should be maintained if it still fits appropriately with the truncated sentence.

If you were to omit words from the middle and the end of sentences in the previous paragraph, your edited text might read:

> "The main purpose of an ellipsis . . . is to indicate the omission of . . . words from a quotation. When the omission occurs in the middle of a quoted sentence, you insert an ellipsis. . . . An ellipsis is three dots . . . with a space before and after each dot."

If you omit one or more sentences from the middle of a quotation, or you leave out the end of one sentence along with one or more sentences that follow, the omission is represented with a period and an ellipsis placed after the last word preceding the omitted text. A longer version of the earlier Barzun quotation illustrates the concept.

ORIGINAL   A good judge of the facts has declared: "All writing is rewriting." He meant good writing, for easy reading. The path to rewriting is obvious: when rereading after a shorter or longer lapse of time what one has written, one feels dissatisfaction with this or that word, sentence, paragraph—or possibly with the whole effort, the essay or chapter. If, as I shall assume, things are not totally bad, the rewriting affects only bits here and there. The criterion is as it has been throughout: Meaning. If words you have set down puzzle you once you have forgotten how they came to your mind, they will puzzle the stranger and you must do something about them—rediscover your meaning and express *it*, not some other or none at all.

ADAPTATION   A good judge of the facts has declared: "All writing is rewriting." He meant good writing. . . . The criterion is as it has been throughout: Meaning. If words you have set down puzzle you once you have forgotten how they came to your mind, they will puzzle the stranger and you must do something about them. . . .

When you take part of one sentence and combine it with part of another, use an ellipsis (without a period), even if you have excluded both partial and whole sentences to form the new sentence. Compare these versions:

ORIGINAL   "Knowing how to use punctuation also augments your credibility. It reflects your literacy and assists you in writing sentences that, in turn, elevate your perceived competence. Too, because so many people have so much trouble with even the simplest of marks, a proficiency in punctuation distinguishes you from the crowd, increasing your worth to nearly any organization or employer."

ADAPTATION   "Knowing how to use punctuation . . . distinguishes you from the crowd, increasing your worth to nearly any organization or employer."

Do not use an ellipsis to indicate omitted material coming before or after what you quote. Because you would seldom quote an entire work, readers will reasonably assume that additional text may have preceded or followed your quoted material.

When you weave parts of a quotation with your own words to form a seamless passage, you need not replace the omitted material with ellipses. Similarly, an ellipsis is not required before or after a quotation comprising only a word or a short phrase. The summary that follows, which combines parts of the first four paragraphs of this chapter, demonstrates both conventions.

The author argues that punctuation enables you to "structure and explain your sentences, allowing your audience to understand more easily what you mean." Effective punctuation, he says, "leads to powerful sentences that, beyond being correct and understandable, drive home your message." A knowledge of punctuation "distinguishes you from the crowd" and makes you more valuable "to nearly any organization or employer."

When your quoted text contains an ellipsis that appears in the original version, the ellipsis is maintained. *"As she looked up from her well-worn APA style guide, she caught the gaze of a studious-looking gentleman staring at her . . . might he be the perfect man or was she just hallucinating under the pressure of learning how to use ellipses"* (Goodwin 22).

If you add your own ellipses to those in the original text, you must differentiate one from the other. MLA gives two options. You can indicate the distinction at the end of the quotation. *"As she looked up from her well-worn APA style guide, she caught the gaze of a studious-looking gentleman staring at her . . . might he be the perfect man or was she just hallucinating . . ."* (Goodwin 22; first ellipsis in orig.). (When your quotation ends with an ellipsis and is followed by a citation source, the period ending the sentence comes after the parenthesis.) Or you can bracket your ellipses. *"As she looked up from her well-worn APA style guide, she caught the gaze of a studious-looking gentleman staring at her . . . might he be the perfect man or was she just hallucinating [. . .]"* (Goodwin 22). When your quoted text ends with the *author's* ellipsis, no period follows the sentence. *"She had heard of a radical way of mastering the comma so controversial it had been banned in five countries, but could she really do it . . . would she truly have what it takes . . ."*

The use of ellipses, as shown, allows you to adapt quotations to more efficiently support your objective. A secondary, less common purpose of an ellipsis is to indicate theatrical pause, reflection, or incomplete thought. When you use an ellipsis in this way and it ends the sentence, no sentence-ending period is necessary.

- Strangely, he often confused the semicolon with the dash as if, unbeknownst to everyone, they were in some incredible way . . . actually alike?
- From the corner of my eye, I noticed her . . . was she really highlighting her APA style guide . . . had I finally stumbled on the perfect woman . . .

- In the dimly lighted room, she told him that if he conquered every punctuation mark she would go out with him, let him hold her hand, and possibly . . . at which point he grabbed his punctuation notes and begin studying.

Slashes

The slash functions in two opposite ways. It pairs words to indicate a choice, such as *yes/no, he/she, pass/fail,* and *win/lose.* In these cases, the slash (with no space before or after) replaces the word *or.* The slash also pairs words to unite them, replacing the word *and,* as seen, for example, in *owner/operator, writer/director, player/coach, washer/dryer,* and *May/June issue.* Sometimes the slash simultaneously speaks to both choice and combination. *And/or,* for example, provides three choices.

By replacing *or* and *and,* words that instantly give secondary status to whatever follows them, the slash more closely unites the two items in the pairing and better establishes their equality. However, the precise meaning of the slash is compromised insofar as it may be unclear whether it replaces *or* or *and,* which helps explain why the slash is less favored in formal writing.

Still, the slash does enable you to avoid certain bulky constructions. It is easier to read *The main ideas/main arguments and subideas/subarguments are . . .* than *The main ideas or main arguments and subideas or subarguments are . . .* The slash can even enhance clarity. *You must specifically and precisely forecast what you are about to describe/explain or argue . . .* speaks of two options. *You must specifically and precisely forecast what you are about to describe or explain or argue* suggests three.

Slashes (with a space before and after the slash) separate lines of quoted poetry when they are short enough to be included in the text, rather than separated into a block quotation. *In her poem, "A Word Is Dead," Emily Dickinson contrasts one view of language—"A word is dead / When it is said, / Some say"—to that of her own: "I say it just / Begins to live / That day."**

The slash is also used with dates (12/25/89; 2010/11), but only in informal communication; fractions (3/4; 9½); URL addresses (http:// RichardKallan.com); and abbreviations (A/C; c/o; $45/oz.).

DASHES, PARENTHESES, AND BRACKETS

Dashes

A dash (also known as an *em* dash) is the equivalent of three consecutive hyphens with no space before or after the dash. Only a question mark, an exclamation point, a closing quotation mark, or a parenthesis can precede a dash; generally, only an opening quotation mark can follow a dash.

A dash usually highlights information that it is not central to the meaning of the sentence. This information can be set off by commas or parentheses, but the dash underscores the point because it is so interruptive. The dash is

---

**The Poems of Emily Dickinson,* Thomas H. Johnson, ed., Cambridge, MA: The Belknap Press of Harvard University Press, copyright © 1951, 1955, 1979, 1983 by the President and Fellows of Harvard College.

more attention grabbing than those forms of punctuation—more "energetic and impetuous," says Karen Elizabeth Gordon in *The New Well-Tempered Sentence*. Thoughts set off by dashes within a sentence are particularly arresting because the dash-text-dash structure briefly stops, starts, and stops the reader. Note, for example, how "really loved" can be punctuated with increasing degrees of interruption/emphasis in this sample sentence:

- He loved, really loved, using dashes.
- He loved (really loved) using dashes.
- He loved—really loved—using dashes.

In addition to emphasizing restatement, as seen here, the dash can draw attention to definition, explanation, abrupt change in thought, or editorial comment.

- She knew how to use end punctuation—periods, question marks, and exclamation points (but not ellipses)—better than anyone in the class.
- Her writing skills helped her achieve phenomenal success—from being CEO of a giant software company to becoming president of a major university and then U.S. senator—until she decided to leave it all and teach remedial English in her hometown.
- She would lay awake, wondering whether her third husband—or was it her fourth?—had ever learned the difference between a comma and a semicolon.
- She learned about punctuation from the time she was five—of course, her father by then had already written four books on the subject.

The nonessential information highlighted by a dash can also be an independent clause appearing within the sentence. *His writing became a punctuation-free zone—some called it a sanctuary where periods, commas, and the like never had to appear in public—that complemented his championing of syntactical anarchy.* If not for the dashes preceding and following the second independent clause (*some called it a sanctuary where periods, commas, and the like never had to appear in public*), the sentence would have been a run-on, having fused two independent clauses.

To prevent the misreading of some sentences, use dashes, instead of commas, to set off appositive phrases that contain internal commas.

ORIGINAL   They continued to misuse certain punctuation marks, dashes, parentheses, and brackets, throughout their papers.

REVISION   They continued to misuse certain punctuation marks—dashes, parentheses, and brackets—throughout their papers.

Ever versatile, the dash can also accentuate elements essential to the sentence's overall meaning.

- I felt sorry that he had failed all his classes, lost his scholarship, and was placed on probation—until I learned he had spent nearly the entire semester surfing in Puerto Rico.

- Colons and dashes!—those varmints did me in at the National Punctuation Contest.
- They introduced me to their salvation—an awe-inspiring, majestic book on punctuation.

Although the word groupings that follow dashes and colons usually differ structurally, sometimes a colon can substitute for a dash. In such instances, you may still choose a dash because it is more dramatic than a colon. The dash, however, is more informal than a colon and easier to overuse, which can lead to a jerky, disjointed message.

Parentheses

Parentheses enclose information incidental or less relevant to your main text. Compared to the parenthetical material set off by commas and dashes, the information enclosed by parentheses is the least essential; only the explanatory footnote is more parenthetical. Parentheses, always used in pairs, signal the presentation of detail worthy enough to include, but not important enough to coexist equally, with the rest of the message. Yet parentheses also create more interruption—thereby giving more emphasis to the enclosed text—than do commas. To be sure, parentheses have a split personality.

Positioning information parenthetically can help subordinate ideas, resulting in a more coherent message that better reflects the writer's key points. Take these two passages, one with parenthetical information, the other without:

- Parentheses can be a helpful writing tool. The singular of *parentheses* is *parenthesis*. However, parentheses should not be overused. Parentheses are my favorite form of punctuation.
- Parentheses (singular, *parenthesis*) can be a helpful writing tool. However, parentheses (my favorite form of punctuation) should not be overused.

In the example given, parenthetical information takes the form of explanation and editorial digression, which, although not crucial to the functioning of the sentence, is helpful and interesting. Here are further examples of how parenthetical comment can add sentence value:

- Parentheses (from the Greek word *parentithenai*, meaning to put aside) should not be confused with brackets.
- In Great Britain (England, Scotland, and Wales), brackets are called *square brackets*, and parentheses are referred to as *round brackets.*
- Many of my college friends (for example, Don, Ed, and Bob) do not care as much about parentheses as I do.
- Most members of the National Council of Teachers of English (NCTE) know a thing or two about parentheses.
- My last boyfriend (now in custody for impersonating a college student) was definitely parentheses challenged.

Use parentheses (a pair) to enclose numbers or letters that label items in a list within your text. Avoid using a single parenthesis, which 1) does not fully enclose its contents and 2) looks like it is missing something.

Numbers or letters that introduce columnized lists need not be placed in parentheses. Sufficient visual separation exists between the number or letter and the text that follows.

ORIGINAL	REVISION
(1) Stanford	**1.** Stanford
(2) University of California	**2.** University of California
(A) Stanford	**A.** Stanford
(B) University of California	**B.** University of California

When parentheses appear within a quotation, they signal parenthetical comment by the author of the quotation. Any commentary (or reference citation) *you* make within the quotation must be bracketed or placed in parentheses immediately following the quotation.

Brackets

When you need or want to comment within the body of a quotation, place your words in brackets. Bracketed commentary offers immediate explanation and clarification.

- His autobiography began unusually: "While at Oxford, I learned how to use round brackets [also known as parentheses]."
- "They [his classmates at Oxford] thought I did not know how to use them [brackets], but I would later show them all."

At times, you may feel compelled to editorialize. For example:

- According to her mom, "Gail [now 19] has loved brackets for more than twenty years."
- Last November, Gail said, "Brackets are my favorite form of punctuation [in October, the ellipsis was her favorite]."

Other times, you will want to let your reader know that an obvious error was the original author's, not yours. *The editor wrote that I needed to fix "all the instances where you're* [sic] *use of contractions is incorrect."* Lest you appear petty, however, use *sic* selectively to acknowledge only the most striking of errors.

Parenthetical information that appears in material within parentheses should also be bracketed. *"Nearly 70% of all college students misuse brackets* (Journal of Bracket Research 24.7 [2010]: 63)."

When you shorten or grammatically revise a quotation to fit your purposes, use bracketed wording to ensure your edited text is coherent.

ORIGINAL	"A paper graded in pencil connotes a less foreboding instructor whose comments and suggestions seem more advisory than absolute. Easy on the ego, the penciled critique is most fitting when reviewing the work of colleagues with whom you want to remain friends.
ADAPTATION	"A paper graded in pencil . . . seem[s] more advisory than absolute . . . [and] is most fitting when reviewing the work of colleagues with whom you want to remain friends."

7 Writing Nonobnoxious Professional and Personal E-Mails

The permissive culture of e-mail does not prompt many guidelines for its usage. Nevertheless, you can produce more readable and persuasive e-mail by heeding certain tips.

SUBJECT: Tips for producing professional and personal e-mails

1. Include a subject line, like the one above, which summarizes the purpose of your e-mail. If you were to say *professional and personal e-mails*, it would not be as effective because it would merely state your topic, rather than abstract your purpose. *Producing professional and personal e-mails* would be better. But because it, too, is not as specific as *Tips for producing professional and personal e-mails*, it would not be as helpful.
2. For longer e-mails, state your purpose in a single sentence positioned somewhere in your first paragraph. At first, this will take a little getting used to, but after a while it will become routine.
3. For longer e-mails, provide a preview or summary statement of the main ideas or main arguments you will be presenting in the body of your e-mail. Place the preview at the end of your first paragraph.
4. Keep your paragraphs short. Shorter paragraphs are easier to read, especially on a computer screen.
5. Skip two lines between paragraphs. The addition of this white space aids readability because it provides places for the eyes to momentarily rest before moving on. It also clearly separates the paragraphs, and, hence, the ideas or arguments.
6. When possible, bottomline each paragraph. In other words, summarize the paragraph's main idea or main argument in a single sentence that starts the paragraph.
7. Label your main ideas or main arguments. Let the reader know when you are introducing your first, second, and third idea or argument.

8. Capitalize the first word of each sentence and all proper nouns. using all lower case affects readability because it is disorientating. we expect a sentence to begin with a capital letter because that is the way we do it in every other writing venue. a capital letter signals the start of a sentence; without it, something seems left off. and how bizarre is it to see *I* written as *i*?

9. Leave one space after sentences. Just like at the start of this sentence.Not like the start of this one. The standard now is to leave one space after all punctuation, including periods, question marks, exclamation points, and colons.

10. Use all upper case (capitals) sparingly. UPPER CASE SENTENCES, LET ALONE UPPER CASE PARAGRAPHS, ARE DIFFICULT TO READ, AS YOU CAN SEE, OR DID YOU ALREADY STOP READING? You also come across as if you are shouting at your reader. A better way to emphasize key words or phrases is by bolding, italicizing, or underlining them; or you can use a larger point size. Having said that,

11. Use **bold**, <u>underlining</u>, *italics*, and *different type faces* sparingly. When overused, they are distracting.

12. Consider using either Georgia (serif) or Verdana (sans-serif) as your default typeface. Developed by Microsoft specifically for computer screens where typefaces, notably serif typefaces, can be harder to read, Georgia and Verdana offer superb onscreen readability owing mostly to all their letters being wider and their lower case letters being taller (particularly with Verdana) than other typefaces.

13. Avoid somewhat generally vague ideas, like this one.

14. Avoid gross overstatement in business communication, unless you like spending time with lawyers.

15. Avoid writing stuff that is like really informal, let alone sexist or racist, because it can turn out to be a real bummer for your readers and will likely have you meeting with the lawyers again.

16. Check for spelling and typographical errors. E-mail is more informel than other writtting venues, but it is not a literrary pigsty. No one wants to read sententences liake the last two. Messages riddled with typos slow your readers and distract their attention. Like accidents on the side of the road, errors cause readers to reduce speed and wonder what happened. Readers, granted, are more accepting of typos in e-mails, particularly when they come from someone they respect and trust because of the professional or personal relationship they share. But if you are e-mailing someone for the first time, you need to put your best foot (text) forward because your readers do not know you well enough to excuse the dozen errors in your 28-word e-mail.

17. Try not to copy (*cc*) everyone you have ever known. In the heat of spirited debate, many remain convinced that promiscuous cc'ing has the power to intimidate because it warns the reader that some very, very important people are going to see what is going on and then you are

going to be in big, big trouble. In the end, cc'ing scares no one and proves to be a counterproductive strategy more apt to escalate than resolve conflict.

18. Reconsider your use of personal logo attachments. They consume space, misdirect the reader's attentions, and are generally unnecessary.

19. Beware of inspirational taglines. You have seen them: *May the powerful winds of destiny forever be at your back in all your endeavors. Let the butterflies of hope lift your spirits to freedom. May you find peace in the pieces of your existence that complete the puzzle of your life.* Inspirational taglines add extra reading time, are not on topic, and can seem like preaching. Understandably, not all readers find them charming.

20. Include your signature file at the end of your e-mail. Make sure it includes your full name, title, business and e-mail addresses, phone number and extension, fax number, and any other data that will make it easier for your reader to contact you. Because the signature file provides your full identification, it also allows for the more personal touch of closing an e-mail with your first name, without having to worry whether your relationship has quite reached a first-name basis.

21. Know when it is best *not* to e-mail your audience, such as in these situations:

When you are angry

Controlled passion gives vigor and soul to your writing. But when you are angry, you are more prone to say things that will prolong the problem and later cause you regret. Even if you are right, a strident tone can damage your image and credibility. The written outburst becomes a permanent record, stored in the arsenal of savvy foes. Let your anger subside a bit before you take fingers to keys.

When you are conveying highly personal or sensitive information

Sometimes anything other than an oral, face-to-face meeting seems cold and removed. You should not e-mail your decision to lay off a longtime, loyal employee for the same reason you would not end a relationship by sending a text message. Discerning communicators care enough about others to know when only human contact will do. In sensitive matters, they will meet with the person face to face, even if only a written report is required, and they are mature enough to think twice about saying anything in an e-mail they would be hesitant to say face-to-face.

When you are facing time-consuming writing

Some e-mails seem to take forever to write, notably when you are asked to explain complex material or answer several lengthy questions. In these cases (excepting, of course, legal requests for documents), it is usually faster to *talk* to the people involved. Information can be questioned and clarified immediately, minimizing the need for follow-up e-mails. If you need a written record, you can summarize the conversation in another e-mail.

When you are speaking off-the-record

If you want to communicate off-the-record, orally express your position in private, not in an e-mail.

8 Why You Are Not Always Read: Rating Your Readability

In the 1920s, educators began developing readability formulas as a way of determining suitable reading books for different grade-school levels. They showed how tabulations of word and sentence length could measure writing complexity and thereby predict whether readers would understand what they read. Early readability formulas, however, were too complicated and tedious for everyday use.

In 1944, Robert Gunning developed a simple, quick, and reliable way to measure writing complexity, called the Fog Index[sm] scale. The Fog Index[sm] score represents the approximate years of schooling *theoretically* needed to comprehend, with 90% or better accuracy, a passage of writing. Texts with lower scores are easier to read and understand than texts with higher scores.

Fog Index[sm] scores reflect the reading grade level, not the intelligence level, implied by the text. A message written at an eighth-grade reading level does not mean it resembles something an eighth-grader would write. Nor does a message having an 18th grade reading level mean that a college graduate wrote it. A sophisticated, well-executed message may have a low Fog Index[sm] score, while a simplistic, clumsily written text may score high. Similarly, a seasoned reader of modest formal education could have less trouble navigating a densely fogged writing sample than might a freshly minted college graduate.

Keep in mind that the Fog Index[sm] scale is a tool, not a prescription, which works best when you use it from time to time to monitor the complexity of your writing. If your scores are consistently high on everything you compose, take a closer look to see whether all your messages really warrant a similar vocabulary and sentence structure.

FINDING YOUR FOG INDEX[sm] SCORE

Pick a writing sample of at least 100 words, ending with a period. Then, follow these steps:

1. *Figure Your Average Sentence Length (ASL).* Divide the number of words in your sample by the number of sentences. Treat independent

clauses—word groupings within a sentence that can stand alone—as separate sentences. For example, *We studied; we learned; we improved* counts as three sentences, even when commas, semicolons, or dashes are used instead of periods to separate the independent clauses. Hyphenated words (twenty-five), numbers (895,000), and dates (2012) count as one word (*June 22, 1916* = three words).

2. ***Determine Your Percentage of Polysyllabic Words (PPW).*** Count the words of three syllables or more. Do not count capitalized words, including the first word of each sentence, or verbs made into three syllables by adding *-ed* or *-es* (such as *created* or *trespasses*). Divide the number of words of three or more syllables by the word length of your sample. This determines your percentage of polysyllabic words. For example, 16 long words in a 130-word sample is equal to 12.3%. Treat this percentage as a whole number when you add it to your average sentence length.

3. ***Add ASL to PPW and Multiply the Total by 0.4.*** Round up the result to the nearest one-tenth percent. Take these two examples:

13.50	ASL (135 words ÷ 10 sentences)
+	
6.67%	PPW (9 polysyllabic words ÷ 135 words)
20.17	
(×) 0.4	
8.068	Fog Index^{sm} score: **8.1**

16.25	ASL (195 words ÷ 12 sentences)
+	
10.77%	PPW (21 polysyllabic words ÷ 195 words)
27.02	
(×) 0.4	
10.808	Fog Index^{sm} score: **10.8**

Fog Index^{sm} scores are useful, but they do not tell the whole story. They measure neither a text's unity nor its coherence. They simply map your word and sentence length, two key ingredients in determining readability. Readability, however, as shown, is influenced by many other factors, such as how well you develop, structure, and format your message. No matter how short your words and sentences, your message will not be easy to read if it is badly forged, poorly organized, or visually unappealing.

PUTTING THE FOG INDEX^{SM} SCALE TO WORK

The revisions of the three examples that follow show how their Fog Index^{sm} scores—and their lengths—can be cut.

Original Fog Index^{sm} Score: 22.3

A **disposition** toward the **encouragement** and **exercise** of **cogency** in **composition** has prompted **publication** and **distribution** of this book.

19.00	ASL (19 words ÷ 1 sentence)
+	
36.84%	PPW (7 polysyllabic words ÷ 19 words)
55.84	
(×) 0.4	
22.336	Fog Index^{sm} score: **22.3**

Revised Fog Index^{sm} Score: 8.1

The goal of this book is to help you write more **cogently**.

12.00	ASL (12 words ÷ 1 sentence)
+	
8.33%	PPW (1 polysyllabic words ÷ 12 words)
20.33	
(×) 0.4	
8.132	Fog Index^{sm} score: **8.1**

Original Fog Index^{sm} Score: 27.2

Despite the fact that the time required for **improving** your writing skills may seem **excessive** at the **beginning**, it will pay **dividends** in the long run **insofar** as once a **reasonable** degree of writing **proficiency** is achieved, it will **appreci-ably** improve your course grades and **dramatically** enhance your sex appeal.

50.00	ASL (50 words ÷ 1 sentence)
+	
18.00%	PPW (9 polysyllabic words ÷ 50 words)
68.00	
(×) 0.4	
27.20	Fog Index^{sm} score: **27.2**

Revised Fog Index^{sm} Score: 7

At first it will seem to take **forever** to improve your writing skills. But once you do, it will greatly improve your grades and enhance your sex appeal.

14.00	ASL (28 words ÷ 2 sentences)
+	
3.57%	PPW (1 polysyllabic words ÷ 28 words)
17.57	
(×) 0.4	
7.028	Fog Index^{sm} score: **7**

Original Fog Index^{sm} Score: 17.2

There are any number of **companies** that offer writing workshops that have as their **ultimate** purpose to train **individuals** how to write better. Through one's **attendance** at these workshops, one can achieve an **enhancement** of **personal** writing skills. This is **important** because success in almost any field of **endeavor** can be **accomplished** on a **regular** basis if one writes well.

But **improving** writing skills requires the **willingness** to **undertake** the **commitment** to working hard on one's writing, and, **unfortunately**, the **decision** to confront one's writing **difficulties** is something that many **individuals** won't accept because they **mistakenly** think they **already** write **terrifically**. Consequently, they are not **receptive** to **receiving instruction** in their writing efforts.

$$
\begin{array}{ll}
22.60 & \text{ASL (113 words} \div \text{5 sentences)} \\
+ & \\
\underline{20.35\%} & \text{PPW (23 polysyllabic words} \div \text{113 words)} \\
42.95 & \\
\underline{(\times)\,0.4} & \\
17.18 & \text{Fog Index}^{\text{sm}} \text{ score: } \textbf{17.2}
\end{array}
$$

Revised Fog Index^{sm} Score: 8.7

Many **companies** offer workshops that train people how to write better and thus enhance their job **performance.**

Coupled with hard work, these workshops can improve most people's writing skills. Yet many are not willing to put forth such effort because they are in love with their writing and don't think it needs any help.

$$
\begin{array}{ll}
18.00 & \text{ASL (54 words} \div \text{3 sentences)} \\
+ & \\
\underline{3.70\%} & \text{PPW (2 polysyllabic words} \div \text{54 words)} \\
21.70 & \\
\underline{(\times)\,0.4} & \\
8.68 & \text{Fog Index}^{\text{sm}} \text{ score: } \textbf{8.7}
\end{array}
$$

Here is a slightly different, bulleted revision:

Many **companies** offer workshops that train people how to write better and thus enhance their job **performance.**

These workshops can improve most people's writing if they will

- first admit their writing needs help, and then
- **continually** work to hone their skills.

$$
\begin{array}{ll}
10.25 & \text{ASL (41 words} \div \text{4 sentences)} \\
+ & \\
\underline{7.32\%} & \text{PPW (3 polysyllabic words} \div \text{41 words)} \\
17.57 & \\
\underline{(\times)\,0.4} & \\
7.028 & \text{Fog Index}^{\text{sm}} \text{ score: } \textbf{7}
\end{array}
$$

Note: Count each bulleted item, whatever its length, as one sentence. If the bulleted item comprises more than one sentence, count each sentence separately.

A low Fog Index^{sm} score does not always mean your writing is concise any more than a high Fog Index^{sm} score proves the reverse. A Fog Index^{sm} score of 8 is not low enough if the text is still wordy. And a Fog Index^{sm} score that far exceeds 12 is not a problem if the message deals with difficult concepts you could not express as well with shorter words and sentences. One criticism of academic writing is not that the Fog Index^{sm} scores are high, which is to be expected given the complexity of the material explored, but that the scores are so much higher than necessary. Good writing in any context remains free of *needless* complexity.

Fog Index^{sm} is a service mark owned by Richard Kallan.

9 Learning to Write Cogently

Novelists and other dramatists have long extolled the practice of nonfiction writing, specifically journalism, as a way of gaining worldly experience, learning information-gathering techniques, and tightening one's prose style. Describing this idealized career path, journalist-turned-novelist Tom Wolfe writes in *The New Journalism*:

> The idea was to get a job on a newspaper, keep body and soul together, pay the rent, get to know "the world," accumulate "experience," perhaps work some of the fat off your style—then, at some point, quit cold, say good-bye to journalism, move into a shack somewhere, work night and day for six months, and light up the sky with the final triumph. The final triumph was known as The Novel.

Just as the practice of nonfiction writing improves one's ability to craft fiction, so, too, it can be argued, does the reverse hold true: The practice of fictive storytelling leads to a more cogent nonfiction writing style.

One unique way of experiencing the benefits of dramatic writing is by composing 55-word short stories. Because the form is so brief, its successful completion mandates the writer's scrutinizing of every word used, as well as the questioning and analyzing of every sentence's function. What is 55-word storytelling, and how can it improve your writing?

HISTORY AND STRUCTURE OF SHORT FICTION

The 55-word short story belongs to a category of *brief* fiction, ranging in length from 55 words to 1,750 words, which has been called various names, including "short shorts," "short short stories," "sudden fiction," "flash fiction," "microfiction," and "fast fiction." Such fiction, says Jerome Stern in his 1996 edited volume *Micro Fiction*, is "an ancient and honorable form, deeply rooted in the human psyche and in the history of human communities," whose earlier predecessors include anecdotes, jokes, fables, and parables. Although variations of brief fiction have been around forever, the impetus for contemporary efforts, according to Robert Shapard and James Thomas, who edited the 1986 anthology *Sudden Fiction*, can be traced to "the spirit of experiment and wordplay of the 1960s." It was then, recalls Stern, that "writers like Russel Edson and Enrique Anderson Imbert started writing stories only a few lines long, as if to pose the question 'Can a short story be too short to be a short story?'" Thus far, it would appear that 55 words is about the minimum length.

To understand the nature and structure of a 55-word story is to realize first what it is *not*. It is not the familiar soundbite or contracted argument that now floods our airways. Nor is it simply an observation, reflection, perspective, or philosophy on life. All could be found in any story, but none by itself constitutes storytelling. Simply put, a 55-word story is an exceptionally short story having a beginning, a middle, and an end. But it is more.

In *The World's Shortest Stories*, a 1995 collection of 55-word efforts, editor Steve Moss reminds us that all stories, regardless of length, must contain four elements: character(s), setting, conflict, and resolution. The character(s), or the story's actor(s), can be human, animal, or even inanimate. Setting, where the story takes place, might be anywhere, including the recesses of one's mind. Conflict refers to the story's tension (what is happening) and how will it be resolved. Resolution, which completes the story, describes how characters address the conflict; it is the culminating action or nonaction expressed by deeds, words, or thoughts. Examples 9.1 and 9.2, taken from Moss's collection, exemplify the story form.

9.1 Student Example

Bedtime Story *by Jeffrey Whitmore*
"Careful, honey, it's loaded," he said, re-entering the bedroom.
Her back rested against the headboard. "This for your wife?"
"No. Too chancy. I'm hiring a professional."
"How about me?"
He smirked. "Cute. But who'd be dumb enough to hire a lady hit man?"
She wet her lips, sighting along the barrel.
"Your wife."

9.2 Student Example

Like Two Ships *by Chris Macy*
He entered the elevator.
"Ground floor, please," he said.

He sounds nice, she thought, but he wouldn't notice me.

He noticed. He noticed her standing there, eyes straight ahead. But he didn't blame her.

Nice perfume, he thought as they parted, he lightly stroking his disfigured face, she counting the steps to the waiting van.

From *The World's Shortest Stories*, edited by Steve Moss, copyright © 1998, 1995 by Steve Moss, published by Running Press, Philadelphia and London. Permission courtesy of Daniel & Daniel, Publishers.

As is true of all quality 55-word storytelling, these two stories develop character, setting, conflict, and resolution quickly and economically. The opening sentence of each provides the setting (a bedroom; an elevator). A sentence or two later, all characters are introduced (a husband and his lover; two strangers). Both tales build swiftly to their conflict: What will happen to the husband's wife? Will the strangers unite? Only when readers reach each story's last line, albeit the last word, does resolution come: The lover is the assassin, but hired by the wife to kill the unfaithful husband; the lovelorn strangers will not couple because, understandably, they misconstrue the inactions of the other.

The writing of 55-word short stories differs from the authoring of more conventional, protracted literature. Traditional dramatic expressions allow for conceptualizing and "working through" story elements *during* the writing process, but this is not practical when constructing what customarily amounts to a four- or five-sentence story. Nor is it wise: The structural and stylistic challenges of compressing a story into 55 words are daunting enough without the additional burden of trying to discover one's message (the character[s], setting, conflict, and resolution) along the way.

Fifty-five-word storytelling requires its author to envision the entire story before drafting narrative and dialogue. Extensive prewriting produces the purpose and direction needed to execute a form whose brevity is transcending. Successful 55-word authorship begins by grasping the crux of the story: What will happen and why, or, in other words, what will be the story's resolution and its rationale as developed through character, setting, and conflict?

The writing of 55-word stories teaches you how to manage language efficiently. The exercise's objective, which is more about advancing a cogent style than developing creative storytelling skills, can also be met by constructing 55-word stories that are *factually* based. Regardless of how the story's "raw data" are secured, the assignment calls for a frugal and precise expression of thought, whose pursuit garners lessons about cogency the writer experiences firsthand.

STYLISTIC CHARACTERISTICS OF SHORT FICTION

Quality 55-word stories tend to be stylistically characterized by

- active verbs;
- concise, minimally modified language;

- short-worded, short sentences;
- reader-inferred detailing; and
- rhythmic grace.

These characteristics, most of which also hallmark effective nonfiction writing, repeatedly appear in quality 55-word stories because they represent the only viable responses to the form's constraints.

The very process of creating 55-word stories forces its authors to embrace a plain but powerful verb-oriented style easily accessible to the reader. Consider, for a moment, how the 55-word story encourages the use of active verbs. Only by embracing a simple and direct sentence style can one meet the assignment's threshold, 55-word maximum. Creating active voice constructions, instead of their wordier passive counterparts, becomes a vital, ongoing activity rather than something primarily addressed in final editing. Put another way, the 55-word story compels active voice constructions because it is "peak" driven. Practically, it cannot include any of the typical story "valleys" where passive voice flourishes. In *Writing for Story*, two-time Pulitzer Prize–winner Jon Franklin insists that all short stories, whether fictional or factual, are similar:

> As you examine the dramatic rises and falls of a story, the most striking thing is that the valleys, where the images begin to build, are where you find the greatest proportion of passive statements. . . . As the drama builds toward a dramatic crest, the sentence length falls off and the proportion of static verbs drops. . . . As the wave builds . . . [the writer's] latitude diminishes. Now, as ascent becomes steep, the possibility of a misstep increases and the danger grows. Each step, now, carries great risk. . . . Each image must be ever more clear and ever more active.

Because 55-word stories must peak quickly, writing in active voice assumes greater significance and ultimately informs the entire text by reshaping how the writer perceives and presents story ideas.

The brevity of the 55-word story also invites the use of concise language with minimal adjectival and adverbial modification. And because you must develop conflict and resolution rapidly, an action-dependent style featuring short words and short sentences and leaving reasonable inference to the audience often emerges. The "Bedtime Story," for instance, contains 12 sentences having an average length of 4.6 words, while "Like Two Ships" has seven sentences, each averaging 7.9 words. In both stories, "difficult" words (words of three or more syllables, excluding those made into three syllables by adding -*ed* or -*es*), which usually take the form of adjectives and adverbs, account for just 3.6% (two words) of each text.

As might be expected, both stories score well on various readability indexes. On the Fog Index^{sm} scale, the "Bedtime Story" scores a remarkable 3.3, theoretically meaning that it is easy enough to be read and understood by a person with only slightly better than a third-grade education. "Like Two Ships" scores a 4.6.

Quality 55-word stories are also marked by their rhythmic grace. This may surprise those expecting a style dominated by tiny sentences to sound choppy and irritatingly monotonous because it lacks the flow and elegance incurred through artful transition, imagery, and other sentence-extending elaboration. What enables 55-word stories to be different? The answer may rest in the form's solicitation of a tight story structure girded by sentences that follow one another neatly and naturally. It is when short sentences do not build upon one another that they seem discrete. The 55-word story affirms that when you carefully assemble and position sentences, regardless of their length, you can create fluid, stylistically snug prose.

Student Power

By far, he was the worst so-called brilliant professor I ever had.

Disorganized, unfocused, incoherent. He made little sense.

Outraged, I circulated a petition, got 37 students to sign, and presented it to a shocked dean.

A year later, he worked a reduced teaching load. Sweet victory?

Today, he died of a brain tumor.

Although 55-word stories are not characterized stylistically by any specific punctuation, they reward the use of certain marks that students usually underemploy. The 55-word story author profits by knowing, for example, that the semicolon can replace the coordinating conjunction between independent clauses, thus saving a word or two, and that the colon can dramatically introduce and emphasize ideas, as well as move the narrative along by facilitating a repetitive structure that eliminates the need for transitional material, as seen in this example:

What Every Teacher Knows

The essay exam: Only Smith, Jones, and Johnson got A's.

The multiple-choice exam: Only Smith, Jones, and Johnson got A's.

The oral exam: Only Smith, Jones, and Johnson got A's.

The final exam: Took the papers, flung them high in the air, and gave A's to only those that never came down. Three didn't.

The writer who practices 55-word storytelling in conjunction with learning about punctuation comes to realize that a valuable payoff results from knowing, for example, how to use commas to avoid confusion over meaning, question marks (after rhetorical questions) to drive home a point, dashes to highlight parenthetical thought, and ellipses to save words and indicate pause. Far from hindering creativity, knowing punctuation aids the process. Concludes Lajos Egri in *The Art of Dramatic Writing*: "There is no conflict between personal approach and basic rules. If you know the principles, you will be a better craftsman and artist."

A SHORT CONCLUSION ABOUT SHORT FICTION

The 55-word short story form prompts you to interact with your text in ways you seldom, if ever, do. You are afforded an immersive exercise that asks you to study, evaluate, and remedy your writing. Continually, you must determine whether your stylistic choices function effectively and efficiently. The experience emphasizes the power, versatility, and richness of language to both inform and persuade. Practitioners begin to recognize the might of cogent expression.

Forcing you to stretch your writing proficiencies and produce concise, tightly structured prose, the 55-word short story exercise proves most beneficial when you struggle with its completion, when you find yourself confronting and critically viewing your writing from every angle in hopes of meeting the challenges of the form. The process makes you a better writer even if you do not finish all your stories. And if somewhere along the way you become so smitten by the lure of fictive prose that you decide to forsake your career and head for that proverbial shack to write the Great American Novel? You, too, will have benefited from the exercise.

Source: excerpts on page 135 from Kallan, Richard, TEACHING JOURNALISTIC COGENCY WITH 55-WORD SHORT STORIES, JMCE, Autumn 2000 (55/3), pp. 81-88. Reprinted with permission.

EXERCISE ANSWERS

Chapter 2

Exercise 1

additional ....more
altercation.....................fight, dispute
anticipate ....expect
approximately..............about
assistance ....help
commitment................promise
compensate ....pay
culminate......................end
encounter......................meet

equivalent...................equal, same
fundamental...............basic
maintenance...............upkeep
necessitate...................require
proficiency..................skill
recollection ....memory
subsequent ....next
sufficient ....enough
terminate ....end

Exercise 2

The director asked Dr. Renovation to conduct a series of workshops on how to make company writing more readable. By Monday, the director would like all managers to send her samples of their typical writing. She will forward them to Dr. Renovation for comment.

Exercise 3

at an early date ....soon
for the reason that ....because
has the ability to ....can
in large measure ....largely
in the near future.........soon
in the vicinity of...........near
is a representation of...represents
is an indication of........indicates
is based on the
    inference ....infers

it is evident that.........evidently
it is probable that.......probably
most of the time.........usually
offers the suggestion...suggests
on a regular basis ......regularly
on the increase ....increasing
performs the
    function of ....performs
take the place of.........replace
to a large degree ....largely

Exercise 4

  A. Show me the money!
  B. I am going to make him an offer he can't refuse.
  C. I'll be back.
  D. Is that your final answer?
  E. So you think you can dance?

Exercise 5

Examples of 55-word short stories appear in Chapter 9.

Chapter 3

Exercise 1

A. I object to your proposal for five reasons.
B. I have never come to class late intentionally.
C. Here are my responses to your ten questions.
D. No social dating websites are devoted to matching Christians, Jews, and Muslims who share a mutual interest in writing clearly, concisely, and compellingly.
E. Some sentences may need to start with *there are*, but this is not one of them.

Exercise 2

My last paper deserved an A+. I developed and structured my arguments flawlessly; I also sequenced them beautifully. And I punctuated my paper perfectly. Most of all, my essay captured my personality: thoughtful, organized, detailed, and modest.

Exercise 3

At first, I thought I was not liked by my professor because she insisted my writing skills needed to be improved. Several ways how I could get better were suggested by her. All her advice was followed. My writing skills were improved, and I was taken more seriously by several employers. Although one or two job offers were received by most of my friends after graduation, I was offered a job by five companies. Because of my strong writing skills, I was just promoted again by my current employer. Now I think I was liked by my professor.

Exercise 4

A. By next week, the school will decide whether to investigate its athletic program.
B. You must pay your parking fines.
C. The play, now six hours long, needs to end.
D. Sharon has consistently won our Writer of the Month award.
E. Students who know how to fix nominalized verbs should assist those who don't.

Exercise 5

I am sorry to hear that many of you cannot attend our annual holiday party, scheduled for the evening of December 24. We had hoped that everyone would have the chance to get together and join in the holiday spirit.

   If many of you would still like to come to the party but cannot attend on December 24, we can reschedule it for December 10. If this date works for you, please let us know.

I look forward to doing all we can to ensure a well-attended, successful holiday party.

Chapter 4

Exercise 1

A. Social networking sites have caused more harm than good.
B. This paper describes the characteristics of an economic recession.
   Or
   This paper explains what causes an economic recession.
   Or
   This paper traces the history of economic recessions.
C. Knowing Latin is advantageous.
D. This tutorial explains how to register for general education courses.
E. The national minimum drinking age should be lowered to 18.
F. Our college should ban alcohol on campus.
   Or
   Our college should not ban alcohol on campus.
G. This report traces the causes of plagiarism on college campuses.
   Or
   This report traces the causes of classroom incivility on college campuses.
H. Cell phone use in public places should be prohibited.
   Or
   Cell phone use in public places should be regulated.
I. Our college should provide more financial aid opportunities to students.
   Or
   Our college should provide more tutoring services to students.
J. I am qualified for your advertised entry-level position in Public Relations because of my education and job experience.

Exercise 2

1. **(B)** The company should give Bill a raise.
2. **(D)** The meal was great.
3. **(C)** The Wildcats will win the league championship.
4. **(B)** The American Popular Culture course was challenging.
5. **(A)** The Office of Productivity is managed inefficiently.

Exercises 3, 4, and 5.

Correct answers will vary.

Chapter 5

Exercise 1

Correct answers will vary.

Exercise 2

When we study law, we are not studying a mystery but a well-known profession. **The law is reason free from passion [Aristotle].** We are studying what we shall want in order to appear before judges, or to advise people in such a way as to keep them out of court. The reason why it is a profession, why people will pay lawyers to argue for them or to advise them, is that in societies like ours the command of the public force is intrusted to the judges in certain cases, and the whole power of the state will be put forth, if necessary, to carry out their judgments and decrees. **Law without force is impotent [Edmund Burke].** People want to know under what circumstances and how far they will run the risk of coming against what is so much stronger than themselves, and hence it becomes a business to find out when this danger is to be feared. **It is dangerous to be right on matters on which the established authorities are wrong [Voltaire].** The object of our study, then, is prediction, the prediction of the incidence of the public force through the instrumentality of the courts. **In a government of laws, existence of the government will be imperiled if it fails to observe the law scrupulously [Louis Brandeis].**

Exercise 3

First sentence: *To what extent can criminal trials be expected to establish the truth about historic events for journalists?*

> **E.** The question is a serious one, but it has been confounded by a discrepancy that exists between the legal and journalistic expectation of what a trial does.
>
> **B.** In law, the purpose of a criminal trial is to decide, according to predetermined rules, whether a defendant is guilty or not guilty of a particular charge.
>
> **D.** Adversary proceedings are designed to render a simple yes-or-no answer to some precise question, a question which has been drawn in as specific a manner as possible.
>
> **A.** In the popular imagination, however, a trial performs a somewhat grander service.
>
> **F.** It is looked upon as a fact-finding operation, an occasion for the public exposure of all known information regarding a given crime.
>
> **C.** The general assumption is that, if fairly conducted, a trial will yield the whole truth; aside from meting out justice to the accused, it will provide complete information and resolve the doubts of a concerned public.

Exercise 4

First sentence: *Nobody ever discovered ugliness through photographs.*

> **C.** But many, through photographs, have discovered beauty.
>
> **E.** Except for those situations in which the camera is used to document, or to mark social rites, what moves people to take photographs is finding something beautiful.

B. (The name under which Fox Talbot patented the photograph in 1841 was the calotype: from *kalos*, beautiful.)

D. Nobody exclaims, "Isn't that ugly! I must take a photograph of it."

A. Even if someone did say that, all it would mean is: "I find that ugly thing . . . beautiful."

Exercise 5

D. The scientist is one of the cultural heroes of our age.

C. He is consulted by senators, courted by corporations, and exalted by the popular mind.

B. It is no wonder that we respect the office of scientist, for one mystery after another has yielded to the formidable machinery of scientific method.

F. And with the mysteries, so also numberless human afflictions are closer to our control: hunger and squalor, pain and neurotic anguish, enervating toil and terrifying superstition, perhaps, as Bergson once dared hope, even death itself.

A. Having, as it sometimes seems, the key to the universe in its very techniques of investigation, science is on a progress of discovery that has no conceivable limit, unless it is the mushroom cloud on the horizon.

E. The triumphs of science seem inexorable as the tide.

ABOUT THE AUTHOR

Richard Kallan (Ph.D., Northwestern University) chairs the Department of Communication at California State Polytechnic University, Pomona. He has taught writing and speaking courses for more than 30 years, including stints at the University of Southern California (USC Marshall School of Business) and the University of California, Santa Barbara (Writing Program). Over the years, he has taught a variety of courses, spanning four disciplines: communication studies, journalism, English, and business.

In addition, Kallan works with businesses, corporations, and government agencies by offering on-site workshops on writing and professional speaking. His clients have included automobile manufacturers; chemical, insurance, railroad, and utility companies; city and county governments; department stores; hospitals; hotels; law firms; and newspapers.

Kallan is the author of *Armed Gunmen, True Facts, and Other Ridiculous Nonsense: A Compiled Compendium of Repetitive Redundancies* (Pantheon Books, 2005) and the coauthor of *How to Take the Fog Out of Business Writing* (Dartnell, 1994). He has also published scholarly articles in *Communication Monographs, Journalism & Mass Communication Quarterly, Journalism & Mass Communication Educator,* and *Journal of Popular Culture.*